Toward
the
Knowledge of God

by

CLAUDE TRESMONTANT

Translated by
Robert J. Olsen

HELICON PRESS

Baltimore

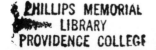

B.
10.
T7

Library of Congress Catalog Card Number 61-14674

Originally published in French in 1959 by Les Editions du Cerf, under the title "Essai sur la Connaissance de Dieu."

Nihil Obstat: EDWARD A. CERNY, S.S., S.T.D.
Censor Librorum

Imprimatur: ✠ FRANCIS P. KEOUGH, D.D.
Archbishop of Baltimore
August 25, 1961

The *Nihil Obstat* and *Imprimatur* are official declarations that a book or pamphlet is free of doctrinal or moral error. No implication is contained therein that those who have granted the *Nihil Obstat* and *Imprimatur* agree with the opinions expressed.

PRINTED IN THE UNITED STATES OF AMERICA BY
GARAMOND PRESS, BALTIMORE, MARYLAND

CONTENTS

How shall we define the word *God?* Does it stand for anything actually pertaining to something real? Or is it merely a word expressing human anxiety and the need to give ourselves a protector, an absolute that will provide us with the peace we desire? If there is anxiety, this alone does not prove that the quest undertaken by human reason in search of an absolute is simply futile. Anxiety can be a motivating factor. But it is reason which must judge, objectively, in the light of its own rational principles—not in order to seek the quiescent effects of an opiate, but to discover the truth, whatever it may be.

What is the significance of the idea or sense of the sacred in "primitive" thought, and in ancient religions, insofar as we are able to examine, understand and interpret them? To what does this idea correspond? Doubtless to feelings of fear, to a need for protection, and to awe and wonder in the presence of cosmic forces. But is there not a latent concept somehow implicit in these vague feelings? As a matter of fact, they are more than feelings. Yet while feelings of fear, desire and awe may produce the idea of the divine, this certainly does not prove that the divine exists. But it does not prove that the divine does not exist, either. Our abhorrence of death does not prove that survival is a fact, nor does it mean that the idea of personal survival is wholly imaginary. We must find grounds for our beliefs.

Is there nothing more than the *world* and *nature?* Is this a self-sufficient world? Is our reason satisfied when we have established the world's existence and discovered the laws that govern this world and its evolution? Is there no other question? Is the question of the "radical origin of things" simply futile and pointless, or is it actually a question that cannot be evaded? Is this a question which merely indicates an ineradicable but illusory requirement of our reason? Or will this demand for ultimate intelligibility find its satisfaction in the fact of existence?

In this inquiry we propose, for our own benefit, to take up once again this eternal question and endless task. We know it is an ambitious project. In the opinion of some contemporary philosophers, it may even seem rather ridiculous. But we do not believe that fundamental questions should necessarily be evaded, as if they were somehow inappropriate. We are convinced, on the contrary, that it is everyone's duty to pose such questions, and that all of us should help others formulate them more precisely.

This essay has no other pretense or purpose than to contribute to the common and inevitable task of research regarding this question, which is also unavoidable: what can we learn about the Absolute? Is there an Absolute, or is there only the world, the contingent, the multiple and the perishable? And if there is an Absolute, what can be said about it? Is the world itself the Absolute? Or if this is impossible for the world, what then might the Absolute be? Can we have any knowledge of it, and how would this be attainable?

We shall try to take nothing for granted as we proceed with this inquiry. Only two requirements will be made: the use of reason and the witness of experience. We shall assume that we are discussing these questions with a man who is willing to use his reason according to reason's norms, and who accepts the teaching of experience.

It may be objected, however, that this is already assuming too much. After all, what do we know about reason's power, or its possibilities and limits? As far as experience is concerned, the whole question is to know what it really represents. Is experience an objective reality or is it only our own representation?

We shall nevertheless suppose that we are holding a discussion with someone who believes in human reason and in objective experience. Our ideal dialogist would be a scientific rationalist who is quite able to make use of reason and who accepts empirical verification, a man who believes that the external world is real and of some importance. A "materialistic" rationalist and scientist would be the interlocutor we prefer.

We cannot enter into discussion with a schizophrenic who doubts the very existence of the external world, the existence of his own body and of everything else, including even his reason itself.

We believe, therefore, that there is a correspondence between reason and experience. However, we shall touch upon the critical problem, and even the ideality of the external world.

Our inquiry will include three parts:

I. Can human thought attain to knowledge of the Absolute, having as its point of departure a consideration of reality, the perceptible and tangible world with all that it contains? In this section we shall exclude one phenomenon among all other phenomena—the phenomenon of Israel—so tiny and inconsiderable from the perspective of space and time.

II. In Part Two we shall turn our attention to Israel. The philosopher owes it to himself not to disregard any phenomenon at all. He readily gives careful consideration to the phenomenon of radium, for instance, and to the rarest phenomena which our experience may present, and these are very often the most significant. Why, then, should he be unwilling to consider the historical phenomenon of Israel? We must try to avoid disappointing the philosopher, however, and must show him that such a local and particular phenomenon may nevertheless contain a lesson of universal import.

In this second section we shall undertake an analysis of the historical and spiritual phenomenon called Israel. But here again, provisionally, we shall make a parenthetical exclusion of a particular phenomenon at the heart of the phenomenon of Israel: one fact among all the facts of Israel's history, the fact of Jesus and Christianity.

III. In Part Three, the last section, we shall consider the person of Jesus, and we shall learn what this man can teach us about the Absolute.

Paris, September, 1958

PART ONE

Knowledge of God Derived from the World

. . . excluding the phenomenon of Israel

Is there nothing more than the world and nature? We may be quite certain of the world's existence, but can we then say that reason is content? Or does another question arise after we have satisfied ourselves about the existence of the world, discovered its laws and analyzed its structure? Can we even conceive of only the world existing, and remain satisfied with the assured fact of its existence, proceeding no farther?

Reason is unyielding in its refusal to be satisfied with the mere demonstration of the fact. We also want to know its ground and cause. But this might be nothing more than a kind of pseudo-question. It can be asked whether our profound dissatisfaction with the establishing of the bare fact may not simply be an inevitable, transcendental illusion which compels us to seek the cause, the sufficient reason, and the foundation of this existence that is apparent to us all.

Is there nothing more than the "world," or is there also an Absolute that is the world's foundation? Here again it may be objected that the very idea of an Absolute which is the abiding foundation of contingent reality is nothing more than a pseudo-concept that rather deceptively conceals our desire for a complete rational explanation which, itself, would be absolute.

Let us eliminate this questionable idea of an Absolute. What will be left to us? There is the perceptible, tangible world which our experience and knowledge are progressively revealing, although we never reach its end in time or its limits in space.

There are two possible hypotheses concerning the temporal existence of the world which must be considered successively: either the world is eternal and never had a beginning, or else the world came into existence a few billion years ago.

The First Hypothesis: the world is eternal, at least in regard to the past, for we are unable to say anything about the future.

But what do we really mean when we speak of the eternity of the world? Today we know the world's history in its broad outlines, and (without presupposing a creator) this could be called the history of creation. We know that man appeared rather recently, and that life made its appearance one or two billion years ago. The earth itself *began* its existence as a bit of matter, probably detached from the sun. If we are told that the world is eternal, this cannot mean that man or life have existed eternally. We have certain knowledge that life, and every living creature, began to exist at a particular time in the world's history. Nor does it mean that our planet is eternal, at least not in its present form, because we are reasonably sure that the earth is the product of a process of evolution or the consequence of an historical accident in the universe. It is therefore the eternity of matter which is meant, for matter is the substratum of all these developments. It is asserted that the existence of this physical matter never had a beginning, and an hypothesis is propounded which maintains that the evolution which we have known empirically is only one of the phases or moments in the eternal history of the universe. We are thus confronted with the image of an eternal cosmic history, conceived as an everlasting palpitation: an endless recurrence of evolutions and involutions, syntheses and disintegrations.

Let us accept this conception of the universe as a hypothesis, although needless to say it has no basis in our experience. But let us accept it provisionally, in order to discover the consequences in regard to the Absolute.

Even according to this hypothesis we find that there is something new which appears at a particular time, whether life, or living creatures, or man. Something more complex, more developed, more alive, more conscious or more intelligent, makes its appearance after a period in which this new synthesis of life did not exist. Something *more* appears following a time when this *more* did not exist.

The *more* appears, but there still remains the whole problem of explaining this something more, this new synthesis and genesis. We cannot explain this addition by the absence which preceded it, unless we renounce the use of reason. We must somehow account for the synthesis of life and the creation of living forms that are increasingly complex, even if we accept the hypothesis of an eternal universe. Reality alone, however, cannot adequately account for this creative process occurring within it.

In any case, the hypothesis of an eternal universe requires us to explain the birth or conception of a child, beginning with two cells, to account for the growth and constitution of the embryo and, finally, the living child. The hypothetical eternity of the universe does not provide any kind of explanation. We cannot explain a *creation* which occurs before our very eyes by what preceded it when this creation was still unrealized.

This is the whole problem, for we are confronted with the fact of a creation that is actually taking place. No matter which hypothesis we accept, when we have ascertained this creative activity in the formation of creatures that did not exist before, human reason must find some explanation for this genesis. It is impossible to account for something new and greater in terms of something lesser. The already existing old cannot satisfactorily explain anything *new* which appears.

We would have to give up the use of reason itself if we tried to limit ourselves to what was previously existing in order to account for the wholly new creation that we see occurring now. The universe, in its formation and continuous creation and gestation, could not be self-sufficient. A growing blade of grass, or a child newly conceived, is quite enough to pose the whole problem. It is certainly unnecessary to make any reference to the "beginning" of the world which, in any case, is not an idea that is accepted by all men. But anything which begins to exist, even in our everyday experience, is enough to present the problem.

We can avoid this insistent question if we claim that everything has pre-existed. This is the teaching of the mysticism of India as we find it expressed in the Upanishads, and of the mysticism of Western civilization originally formulated by Empedocles and in Orphism. This teaching affirms that everything pre-exists. There is no birth, or any beginning of existence. Birth is merely an appearing, an emerging of souls at the level of appearances, and these souls pre-existed in the heart of the One, the heart of the Absolute. Birth is a descent of pre-existing souls, a kind of "fall" into the body.

In this metaphysical theory which denies the empirical fact that existence has a beginning, we find an affirmation of the pre-existence of all beings within the Absolute. There is no metaphysical denial of the Absolute, but rather a repudiation of experience and a denial of creation.

It is consequently impossible to have recourse to a metaphysics of this type in order to deny the Absolute in the name of experience, which is our point of departure. In this inquiry we began with experience as something *given*, and accepted by everyone. We wanted to see if from this starting point we could attain to the discovery of an Absolute. We cannot accept the denial of the fact of creation and of beginnings, which we find in certain metaphysics of identity. Nor can we make use of their arguments to deny the Absolute, for it is exactly because of a certain conception of the Absolute that they reject the universal experience of birth and continuous creation.

The Second Hypothesis: the world had a beginning. This hypothesis is mostly based upon the idea of an expanding universe today. According to this, the universe had a real beginning, and is evolving in an irreversible manner.

In this case, we must explain not only the process of evolution and the genesis of new beings which had no pre-existence (just as with the other hypotheses), but also the "original" beginning. Existence appears, following nothingness. Something, whether matter or energy, begins to be, although nothing precedes, underlies or causes it.

This sudden appearance of being in the midst of nothing-ness, so to speak, is absurdity itself, from the perspective of human reason. It is the supreme example of an irrational idea. However, this absurdity is not essentially different from the facts that were mentioned before. A child is conceived, beginning with two cells; life emerges out of matter; something that did not exist before now begins to exist. The greater appears, and cannot be explained by the lesser. It is this greater and truly wholly new existence which is the universal datum. In the course of time some superior being appears which nothing previously existent can entirely account for.

The hypothesis of an original beginning presents everything in a particularly spectacular way. There is emptiness and eternal nothingness; then suddenly there is being and matter. But this is rationally inconceivable.

Bergson has shown in his famous analyses that nothingness is not merely inconceivable: it has never actually been a concept in our thinking. We never think in terms of nothingness, for the word itself corresponds to no real idea at all. There is always some degree of being whenever we think about nothingness—even if only the being of the subject who, by his thinking, annihilates everything. Consequently, the idea of something exist-ent that "follows upon" nothingness, or suddenly emerges "in the midst" of nothingness, must be a false conception. Being does not come forth from emptiness. Existence cannot be derived from nothing. To maintain that being emerges from nothingness is to assert something that is utterly contrary to reason's most essential requirement, which is rationality itself.

We must therefore fall back upon the hypothesis of an eternal universe in order to avoid this uncaused "emergence" of being out of nothingness. However, while the hypothesis of an eternal world is only hypothetical, with no real basis in our experience, it is a fact that the emergence of being is nevertheless *exactly what we observe continually and universally*, if we keep our eyes open, or simply perceive what is constantly before our eyes. A growing blade of grass, a child who is conceived and born, life which appears at a particular time, the formation of millions of living species, even the conception of an idea or a work of art—all these are only some of the endless manifestations of a continuous creation in which something *new* is constantly appearing which did not exist before. There is therefore an "emergence" of being, not out of "absolute nothingness", but rather in the midst of a reality which does not include (or did not previously include) this something that is born, something real and wholly new, which now makes its appearance. Following upon non-existence, a being appears. The child who did not exist a year ago now exists. This is the fundamental fact, and in so far as the essential point is concerned it is the same, whether we consider the "original beginning" of the world or these wholly new beginnings at every moment, around us and within us.

We live in a world in which creation is the rule. This is the fact. Consequently, to develop the analysis through which we are seeking the absolute ground and cause of reality, we are not obliged to accept the hypothesis of a world that is limited in time. We do not have to think in terms of an "original beginning" of the world. This beginning, or rather these beginnings—constantly occurring at every moment of duration, in which millions of beings are born and begin to exist—are enough to pose the question of the radical origin of all things quite adequately.

Since the hypothesis of a universe that is finite in time and space is not either obvious or certain for all minds, we shall limit ourselves to the indisputable, as being apparent to everyone: the constant and universal initiation of existence at every moment of our lives. And thus we discover a method of approach that was used by St. Thomas in the thirteenth century when he raised the question of the knowledge of God among philosophers, some of whom upheld the idea of an eternal world. Contemporary beginnings are sufficient for us, and we believe that their metaphysical significance is quite as considerable as the original beginning of the world.

But let us conclude this first approach to the problem. The *more* that appears, the *new* which is born, could not be explained by the less, or by the absence or non-existence of this new being. It cannot be explained in terms of anything that is not itself. The creation of a new being which did not pre-exist, cannot be accounted for by anything previously existent.

Bergson, in his analyses of the essence of time, establishes that the essence of real duration has always been this something *new* which indicates a real and fundamental creation. Created reality, *natura naturata*, is not sufficient to account for this creation of new beings that takes place within it and is constantly surpassing it.

Contemporary thought is especially responsive to this vision of a world that is in process of continuous creation. The fact of evolution taken in the widest sense suggests and manifests this continual genesis of fundamentally new beings that did not exist before. This is the most universal datum of experience.

This conception of reality, prevalent during the past hundred years, is in complete contrast, point by point, to the vision proposed to us in the metaphysics of India or of Plotinus. Open minds the world over are in agreement on this revelation of a creative process occurring before our very eyes at every moment, and continuously during billions of years. The question is simply to determine whether or not the creative process implies and requires a creator.

Our thesis, which in our opinion is the expression of rationality in its deepest and most essential requirement, is that the newness of being which appears at any given moment cannot be explained or accounted for rationally by any being or existence which preceded it empirically. The anterior does not contain the ulterior. The greater is inexplicable in terms of the lesser. We must account for the existence of all these fundamentally new beings that appear at a particular moment of time.

It would be a rejection of empirical knowledge if we were to affirm the pre-existence of all beings in some anterior being (as with the metaphysics of India; and, in another sense, implicitly in Marxism, as we shall see). If we should say that all beings pre-existed in the heart of the One, the Absolute, as the Hindu believes, or that thought, consciousness and life preexisted at least potentially in matter (considered as the Absolute), which is the teaching of Marxism, we would then be rejecting the witness of experience, giving up philosophy, and proposing myths.

We exist, we are alive, but our existence and our life are a wonder and a mystery to us all. It is a fact, of course, that we exist, but a fact which we cannot explain. That the whole universe exists is another datum which is not self-explanatory, nor can we account for this fact either. We may study the structure of the universe, and of matter and life, or we may consider their development and evolution, but we are always without the answer to the question of being and existence. The universe is existent, with all the infinite richness of its structure and diversity, its development and evolution. But its very existence seems to be a fact which in itself requires some kind of explanation. Mere verification of the world's existence is not sufficient for us. A question arises in regard to this existence, structure and evolution. It is a fundamental question which concerns the source and origin of this existence.

Is this a pseudo-question, like one of those questions which conceptual analysis or even psychological analysis reduces to nothing and then dismisses like a bad dream? This is what we must now determine.

For the moment let us say only that the missing answer, together with the desire for immortality and a life of blessedness which led men to imagine the existence of gods in a realm of bliss—as well as a fundamental feeling of inadequacy—are summed up in our awareness that existence and life are like a gift that has been bestowed upon us. Our human condition seems definitely to be something imposed. We are not the authors of our own existence, nor of our mortal, suffering and ephemeral condition. If we had been the real authors of our condition and life, we would surely have made ourselves happy and immortal, like the gods of mythology. We would have provided ourselves with everything that we are so sadly lacking. But we did not create ourselves. According to the ancients, it was the gods who fashioned us, those jealous gods who made us fragile and mortal, keeping immortality and the life of blessedness for themselves alone.

Whatever we may think about these ancient legends, it is

certain that we are not self-created. Our existence, our nature, our body and soul, are a perpetual wonder to us and a cause of endless amazement. Biologists analyze the structure of our organism, and yet our knowledge of the human body is still very elementary. Our soul, our psychology, and our tendencies, are quite as mysterious to us. It will require the long and patient labors of science to reveal ourselves as we really are. Our existence, the beating of the heart, the chemistry of our breathing, the digesting of food that will be transformed into ourselves through no effort of our own—even our thinking process, which flows like a fountain whose source is unknown: all constitute a mystery. We are, in fact, an enigma to ourselves. In our own hands we are like a bright new toy that is given to a child who turns it round and round with astonishment. Everything within us has been given: our existence and life, the palpitation of the heart, and even the very thoughts we think, coming from some unknown source, as from a depth we have never fathomed.

The poet tells us that the "I" is *another self*. The philosopher or mathematician may say, "This thought which comes to me and is my own certainly does come as though 'rising in my heart,' as the Hebrews express it, but I cannot definitely say that I am its ultimate creator. Every thought that comes into my mind is also a gift with which I cooperate, a gift which I bring forth from within and conceive in the depths of the self, but it is nevertheless a gift, like my very self, for I am not the creator of this 'I' or this self. I am truly something given to myself."

The energy within me, the motion and strength, the power to act and to think, have been placed in me, but not by myself. I was born and I received. Life and thought, like motion and action, have all been *received* by man. Existing, living, thinking and acting are certainly our own, but at the root of our existence and life, and fundamentally and interiorly in our acting and thinking, there is energy which we did not create.

Some metaphysical philosophers have preferred to reject this immediate datum of our human experience. They refuse to admit that we are in the humble condition of created beings who have received everything and possess nothing that has not been given.

They deny that man is not his own creator. They are not willing
to acknowledge such passivity in man with regard to his existence, life and thought. Man is definitely the creator of himself,
they say, and he is not dependent on any other. And if man
does not seem to realize that he is his own creator, even feeling
rather lost in a world he cannot remember creating, and if he is
humbled in his condition as a creature, it is simply because he
has *forgotten* his true nature, which is actually divine. In fact,
the "self" which the poet regarded as another self, is really the
Absolute. Each of us may say, "I am the Absolute. But I am
no longer aware of this. I have forgotten. And I must now realize
my true nature again, for then I shall clearly discern that I am
the creator, not only of myself, but of the whole world of my
representation."

It is still necessary to explain the difference between the *Self*
which is the Absolute and this empirical and immediate "self"
that does not know, or no longer realizes, that it is the Absolute.
But how could we have forgotten our own divine essence, and
why are we in exile from our true Self? What is the reason for
this fall?

It is a major problem of these same metaphysical philosophers to account for this fall. However, they limit themselves to
a recognition of the fact, or try to justify it in some mythical way
by assuring us that the alienation is a part of the very life of the
Absolute, and constitutes a necessary stage in its gradual evolution. This would be the stage or phase of negativity, soon to be
overcome by a return to identity. The life of the Absolute must
necessarily include this process, this rending and alienation.

In metaphysics of this type, the idea of a creation, not only
of man but of the world as well, is thus repudiated.

If it seems apparent to me that I have received existence,
life, motion and thought, I have even better reason for thinking
that the world as a whole seems incapable of being the explanation of its own existence, its nature and development. The material world cannot give us the explanation because it has no
voice. But man has a tongue to say that the physical world itself
is also something given, and that the animal world and all of life

in its history and diversity are simply here for a while, having a beginning and an end, but not as the creators of themselves.

The universe exists, with all that it contains. It develops and evolves. Life appeared some few billion years ago at most, and also develops and evolves. Living species appear, and some of them disappear. Finally, man enters upon the scene. But matter itself, as physical matter, seems unable, from our point of view, to create either itself or the historical tree of life with all its species. We may apply to the universe as a whole what our analysis revealed in regard to ourselves, who are a very small part of this same universe. We learned that we are a gift to ourselves, so to speak, and that whatever we possess has been received. The same thing may be said of the universe as well. The animal which is without speech is no more the creator of itself than we are. This thing, this tree or stone, this atom of hydrogen, is not self-created either. The universe as a whole is progressively revealed to our perception, with its worlds, systems, galaxies and matter. It offers us no reason to say that it is self-created, or that it can itself provide the explanation of its own existence and of all that it contains, including ourselves. Nothing could justify an attempt to conceive of the universe as a kind of cosmic animal, as Plato assumed, or a decision that this cosmic animal is a god.

The universe is not self-created. It exists, it is present, just as we are also. But we must still cope with the question of this existence and its explanation.

It may perhaps be objected that the existence of the universe requires no metaphysical explanation. Our recognition of the fact of its existence, and of our own existence within it, is quite sufficient for us. Any question concerning this existence is simply futile. The question of causality, for instance, is a pseudo-question, having been posed incorrectly. The problem of the radical origin of things is a false problem. A noetic, psychological or even structural analysis clearly reveals its pointless futility by taking the mechanism of the question to pieces.

As far as the universe is concerned, we shall admit provisionally that we must limit ourselves to ascertaining its actual existence and development, and we shall assume that the question of the cause and radical origin of all things is something forbidden to us.

Let us turn our attention once more to ourselves as a thinking part of the universe. We are not self-created. Our existence, our biological life and even our act of thinking are all a mystery to us. It is useless to say that existence needs no explanation, and that mere discernment of the fact of existence should be sufficient. After all, our existence is a problem to us, for each of us is conscious. We appropriate the gift of existence, life, motion and thought to ourselves, but we must still acknowledge the fact that we are not the authors of this existence, or of the body, or of the power to act and create. We receive all of these gifts which we appropriate to ourselves. But at the root of our being, we are not self-created. If we pose the question of our own existence, it does not mean that we are "emotionally disturbed." Our question possesses objective meaning, or else no question has meaning at all, and in that case we ought to stop thinking entirely.

When we wonder about the source of our existence, recognizing that neither our own nor the existence of the universe as a whole is self-sufficient (having nothing within it to explain or justify its being, and not being self-creative), we are posing a question that is essential to the exercise of human reason. We can refuse to consider questions of this kind, as the positivists urge us to do, but we would then be forsaking a whole area of rational inquiry, refusing to use our reason in accordance with certain demands that are connatural to it. This would be a repression of the constitutive exigency of reason, repelling it and suspending it. But this act of repression would be incompatible with the insistent, inner demand for rationality: a yielding to excessive prudence, or a defeatism of the mind, with no compelling rational justification.

The question of the source of our being, and more generally of the existence of the universe, and the question of the cause of empirical existence, may perhaps seem illegitimate. Does it not lead us into a pseudo-reasoning process? Is causality anything more than a category of our thinking which has validity only in the realm of experience and of appearances? Briefly, the question in regard to being and its sufficiency or insufficiency, as well as with respect to the radical origin of things, may seem to lie beyond the confines that mark and limit the legitimate field of positive thought.

The determination of these very confines, however, needs to be carefully considered. Thought must certainly exercise vigilance over itself, and critical reflection is necessarily an integral part of its rigorous rational exercise. But if we propose a priori limits to human thought, naming boundaries which must not be crossed, it would also be dogmatic and presumptuous. For how can we tell what is possible or impossible to human thought? Are we its creators? The exercise of this thinking process is our own, for we make it ours, but in the source of our thinking there is nevertheless a gift. And what do we know about the structure of our reason?

Perhaps we can learn more about our reason and its powers and limits through a reflective analysis of the exercise of reason. Such an analysis is possible and desirable, but reflective analysis also has its own limits.

Reason is not an organ or a group of organs which may be coldly examined or dissected, so to speak, in order to determine its operation, composition and limits. We are not the creators of this power to think, which is called reason. We only know this power and realize its demands from its use through the course of centuries, when applied to reality. We cannot determine in an absolute, a priori manner what is rational and what is not. It is reality which is the sole judge in this respect. Some things may have seemed irrational at one time which were later considered rational, because of verification.

The roundness of the earth and its rotation around the sun, the antipodes, the origin of species, the wave theory of light, the corpuscular theory, and the synthesis of these two theories in wave mechanics, together with all of the discoveries of science, have revolutionized a certain rationality, or at least a certain presumption of rationality. It seemed quite absurd to say that men were walking about upside down at the antipodes, but this no longer seems absurd to us because we know that they really are doing so, and because we have changed our conception of "up and down." The rotation of the earth around the sun no longer gives us a feeling of dizziness, and we know that one body may move another without touching it. The whole classic conception of causality, based upon the theory of the impact of two billiard balls, simply falls apart as soon as we discover that these two balls, when one brings about the movement of the other, do not actually touch. *As a matter of fact, the rational is whatever exists.*

We no longer predict what may be possible or impossible in science. We know that the whole advance of modern scientific thought has consisted in the overthrowing of the so-called evidence of rationality that was commonly accepted. The essentials of our rationality must not be confused with any particular system of objective rationality of one period or another. We can no longer speak of reason as if it were an organ, or (if we may use the term) as a kind of motor which connects up with reality under certain conditions that can be determined a priori. Reason is not an organon. It is an exigency, but we cannot know the last word about it until we have attained to the completion and consummation of knowledge. What is the nature of reason? This question must remain unanswered until we reach the end of our human quest.

It is therefore better to speak of the need for rationality or for intelligibility rather than reason, as though reason were something clearly defined, whose anatomy is well known. Reason is certainly not a thing that can be dissected.

This position does not imply or entail any scepticism at all in regard to reason, nor any attempt to soften the necessary severity of the need for rationality. On the contrary, it seeks only to prevent a dogmatism more subtle than the naïve dogmatism of the pre-critical era. It keeps us from attempting to transform an exigency into a thing, from determining the a priori limits of our efforts to know what is real, when we should receive such instruction only from reality itself. We shall not know the limits of reason's effort, if there be any limits, until we reach the end of the quest, if there be any end. It is only reality that will tell us what is rational and what is not. Let us be docile towards reality and to whatever it may teach us through the efforts of scientific research. We must not reiterate the naïve interdictions of Auguste Comte concerning certain fields of knowledge.

The Kantian critique, of course, did not impose any prohibitions within the scientific realm. It set the limits at the confines of experimental knowledge. But here again, we must be more prudent and carefully examine the procedure of the Kantian critique.

In the name of rational exigencies that are apparently coherent, the Kantian reason forbids itself to go beyond a certain kind of knowledge which is found strictly within the compass of experience. Kantian reason therefore dogmatizes, at least in its refusal to permit the passing of certain limits. It is dogmatic in claiming that it can describe the transcendental structure of reason and of our understanding and sensibility. It refers to reason as though dealing with an organon. After examining it, the conclusion is reached that it can serve only for empirical purposes, but cannot transcend the order of experience. This is another instance of dogmatism, in this case negative, which serves to prohibit the metaphysical quest, not to invite it. But it is nevertheless an illegitimate and unjustified dogmatism, for how could human reason possibly know a priori the limits of the possible or the impossible when it is not self-created and cannot therefore know its own potentialities in a complete way, especially in view of the fact that the efforts of metaphysical research are only in the tentative, initial stage?

Kant launches into his critique, maintaining that mathematics and logic have both succeeded while metaphysics has failed since it has not won unanimous consent. This is yielding to discouragement prematurely, and it is a very hasty condemnation of a tentative effort, blundering no doubt but which has not been fruitless. It would require another book to set forth the balance sheet of two or three thousand years of metaphysical reflection.

Do we know whether or not human reason can transcend the order of sensible experience in order to affirm certitudes that are not verifiable by the means and instruments of experimental science? This is a question which poses metaphysical problems that Kant seems to consider settled or solved, since he does not elucidate them.

Can human reason, or rather human thought, legitimately engage in reflection and a line of thought that leads to the proposing of truths (i.e., affirmations concerning being and existence) which are beyond the empirical, tangible and visible, and are not subject to experimentation? Kant says no. But for what reason? He does this in the name of a transcendental analysis of the structure of the conscious subject. But how is this analysis carried out? Its point of departure is a particular conception of science, a particular theory of scientific technique and of logic, whose historical sources are clearly apparent. We shall not attempt to make a critique of this transcendental analysis of pure reason here. A very large volume would be needed for that, and every historical analysis could then be examined. We shall limit ourselves more simply to a modest clarification of the presuppositions, apparently unnoticed, which Kant seems to consider as self-evident. These presuppositions underlie his entire critique and determine the conclusions far more definitely than all the subsequent analyses.

We must now face the problem of creation once again. Quite naturally, and apparently without even raising the question, Kant accepts the hypothesis of a human soul, or rather a humid mind, wholly independent and having no relationship with any creator. We shall not call this an hypothesis of self-creation, for this would assume that Kant had considered the problem himself, as the post-Kantians have done in affirming the divinity of the self. But Kant did not take the pantheistic point of view. Nor did he consider things from the perspective of the metaphysics of creation. Some will praise him for this, since he wanted to analyze human reason and examine specifically the question of knowing whether or not reason can propose metaphysical affirmations such as the creation or non-creation of man and the universe. We might concur in this praise and approval of Kant if the position which he adopted were simply a *methodology*—that is to say, if it were simply provisional.

If Kant began by telling us that he intended to study the structure of human reason and its power, that therefore he was excluding any and all metaphysical assertions provisionally, while adopting a position of methodical doubt; if he went on to say that he wanted to see whether he could find a way out of this doubt after making a critical analysis of the power of human reason, we could then allow Kant this legitimate point of departure. We would examine with him the various hypotheses implicit in this Critique of Pure Reason, this provisional exclusion of the metaphysical affirmation, this effort to verify the instrument before making use of it.

However, the parenthetical exclusion itself includes certain hypotheses which are not without importance.

A provisional omission of all metaphysical affirmations rests upon certain possible hypotheses which require elucidation. Either we live in the Absolute, having our existence, motion and thought within it, or else we do not. There is no middle ground. And the provisional exclusion changes in meaning with the one or the other hypothesis. That is, it is impossible to treat the problem of knowledge unless we adopt one of these hypotheses, even though we pretend to accept neither. The soul is either created or uncreated. The whole problem of knowledge is posed in two different ways according to the hypothesis we adopt. It is impossible to avoid the alternative, for we cannot study the structure of human reason or evaluate its power without posing the question of its radical origin. If we wish to omit this question provisionally in order to determine whether human reason is able to decide such questions, we must consider the matter from within this exercise of reason and make an analysis of the modalities. We will be unable to verify the act whereby reason claims to know anything outside itself. We have taken our place within the conscious subject, which is quite legitimate, and we have eliminated the problem of the radical origin of the conscious subject, and this is also legitimate. We can describe the operations of reason, but the parenthetical exclusions will not, of themselves, tell us whether the subject has attained to knowledge of anything other than the conscious subject alone.

After making a methodological exclusion of the question of the conscious subject's radical origin, we cannot determine a priori the transcendental structure of this conscious subject, because the subject is not like a body which can be dissected. The subject's cognitive power can be determined and evaluated only by and within the verified application of knowledge. But we cannot know the limits of this power until we reach the end of our quest for knowledge. And we still have a long way to go. We would be guilty of unjustifiable dogmatism if we set the limits of the conscious subject's cognitive power a priori, as if we knew the transcendental subject quite thoroughly, and this would be possible only if we had created this subject and were self-created ourselves. This hypothesis, however, was rejected for the sake of method, since it is a metaphysical thesis.

There are only two possibilities. It is we who are the creators of the transcendental subject and of ourselves, and we are the Absolute. Consequently, we know enough about the structure and power of the transcendental subject to determine the limits. But if we really are the creators, why would there be any limits for the transcendental subject?

Or else we are not self-created, and in this case how could we make any decision concerning the a priori structure and the conscious subject's power to know before we have embraced the whole range of knowledge in a comprehensive way? It is through pride rather than humility that we would ever try to impose limits on the subject's cognitive power, for we are not the creators, and this would be arrogating to ourselves a decision which can only be made by the creator himself, who alone knows what the created subject can or cannot do. Man, as a created subject who analyzes his reasoning powers reflectively, cannot proceed with his analysis from the perspective of the creator. He can only think methodically about this cognitive power entrusted to him, although he is unable to foresee its limits, because a knowledge of its limits would presuppose a radical knowledge of his nature.

The worker, for instance, knows the object or machine which he has made. His knowledge is radical, total and a priori, for it was he who devised the plan and built the object or machine accordingly. However, man is not a machine fabricated by man, and consequently man is a mystery to himself. This does not mean that man is unknowable to man, but rather that man cannot know himself in the way that the worker or the artisan may know the machine which he put together, piece by piece, and can take apart because of his integral knowledge of its composition. Man does not know his own structure and composition a priori, as the artisan knows the product he has made. Man can only know himself anatomically, physiologically, psychologically or intellectually as an object that he has neither produced nor created. This is also true of the transcendental subject. Man can learn about this subject progressively, as he learns about the structure of his own organism through much effort, which still remains incomplete and inadequate after centuries of study. But man is not able to describe the structure of the transcendental subject a priori, because he is not the artisan of this subject. A priori knowledge about anything can only be possessed by the maker.

Our objection to Kant is that he referred to human reason as if it were a machine whose parts could be dismantled one by one, while measuring its power and evaluating its aptitude for application to reality. But human reason has nothing in common with a machine. It is better to accept the pantheistic hypothesis and say that human reason is uncreated because in a certain sense, still undetermined, it is a part of divine reason, and man is a portion of the Absolute. In this case, the problem of knowledge is resolved by the fact that human reason knows the world and the Absolute, since it has itself produced the world and actually is the Absolute. It is not the problem of knowledge which constitutes the mystery, but rather the problem of the limitation of knowledge, considered as the fall which resulted in our forgetting that we are the Absolute, so that we now need the sage to teach us and the philosopher to remind us. It is the forgetting that constitutes the problem.

However, if we are created beings, the problem of knowledge must be posed quite differently. With St. Paul we would then say, "In the Absolute we live and move and have our being."

Thinking is not a solitary act. We are not isolated in our act of existing, nor in our living, moving, acting or thinking. We are created beings, and this means not only that we were created at a particular moment, but also that we are being created unceasingly. Our existence is sustained and informed by a creative activity. Our act of living, which is our own, does not rest upon ourselves as though we were self-created, but upon an other and within an other. Not a single heart-beat would even be conceivable were it not for the indwelling of this creative life deep within us. The act of thinking, like that of living, is not an act in which we are sufficient unto ourselves, bringing forth all the resources of thought as if from within ourselves alone. Our existing, acting and thinking are certainly our own, but the creative activity is operative in all we think and do. We can cooperate with this creative activity and appropriate this gift of existence, motion and thought to ourselves, or we can reject it. Indeed, each of us can will to become his own demiurge. Nevertheless, no beat of the heart, no thought of the mind, nor any deed of ours, however trivial, is even possible without this immanent operation of creative energy within us, bringing us into existence, bestowing our autonomy, fashioning our biological individuality and our creative personality, rational and free. Later, we shall consider this problem of the grafting of a created freedom, which is creative, upon an uncreated, creative freedom.

But continuing with our consideration of Kant's critique, let us note that he does not explicitly adopt the hypothesis of a created conscious subject, or the contrary hypothesis of an uncreated conscious subject substantially identical with the Absolute. Some of Kant's disciples interpret the doctrine of the critique in the sense of this second hypothesis, as for instance, Fichte. In the pantheistic conception of reality, or more specifically from the perspective of a metaphysical system which teaches the substantial identity of the human self and the Absolute, a consequent and coherent theory of knowledge is possible. The self would actually be the creator of the world of its own representation, knowing and recognizing itself as Absolute, and attaining to the immediate intuition of its own essence by a transformation which turns it away from the illusion of the phenomenal world.

From the perspective of the metaphysics of creation, the problem of knowledge can also be treated coherently without ending in dilemma.

Kant, however, committing himself to neither hypothesis, can find no way to solve the problem of discovering how human knowledge could transcend the ascertainment and description of empirical data.

As a matter of fact, the conscious subject does not find, by interior analysis of the contents of the mind alone, the necessary resources to transcend these data, or any way to know an object or being that lies beyond empirical data. This is because the subject, per se and solitary, could not be the whole explanation of this act any more convincingly than it would be possible for a living man, considered in isolation, to account for the beating of his heart, the least of his deeds, or even his existence, by any mere reference to himself. Kant's critique has proved that on his hypothesis of a conscious subject, considered in isolation, and excluding the condition of created being, metaphysical knowledge cannot be justified. The conscious subject finds nothing in the mind that could justify the act by which the data of experience would be transcended. Let us remember, however, that neither will the conscious subject discover anything by interior analysis that would adequately explain our existence, life, motion or action. For man, considered as solitary, and excluding the creative activity always operative within him which sustains and quickens him, is really nothing, or would be nothing, for he would not exist at all. It is the hypothesis, in this instance, which is simply preposterous. Man cannot conceive of himself in separation from the Absolute, as will be clearly shown. Even Kant's disciples, who interpret the critique in the sense of a new ontology, have placed man back within the Absolute. But they define man's relationship with the Absolute differently from the metaphysics of creation. Fichte, Schelling and Hegel reject the idea of creation, following Spinoza. They must explain the existence of nature, the limitation of the self, the apparent multiplicity of monads, in some way other than by reference to creation, either in terms of an alienation or as a fall.

For the purposes of our present inquiry we should simply keep in mind that Kant's critique cannot possibly inhibit us in our metaphysical quest because it takes for granted the very points that are in question, posing the problem of knowledge in an unrealistic frame of reference. The Kantian conscious subject will not discover the Absolute, because the whole analysis has been carried out with the presupposition that there is no dependence on the Absolute, and that the act of knowing does not originate in the Absolute. But this is exactly what ought to be verified first of all. If it is true that we exist and live and move within the Absolute, the problem of knowledge is posed in a wholly different way, and Kant's critique can only lead us into error. For if there is an Absolute, then we must determine whether the empirical datum that the critique accepts, which is the world of experience, is even possible. The conscious subject certainly exists. But this existence is necessarily created or uncreated. These are the two possibilities that we must consider now. There are *only* two possibilities for metaphysics. There is no middle ground. Either we must turn toward a metaphysics of creation of the biblical type, or else toward a metaphysics which teaches that the self is uncreated. The Upanishads represent the first known type of this latter metaphysical tradition.

Apparently we are enclosed within a circle. We are trying to determine whether the human mind can attain to metaphysical knowledge, and especially whether the idea of the Absolute is meaningful. This lends us to the critical problem of knowledge. The latter, in its turn, directs our attention back to certain metaphysical presuppositions. We cannot pursue our metaphysical inquiry unless we find an answer to the critical question. However, this question itself can only be treated on the basis of metaphysical presuppositions. We cannot even consider the problem of knowledge, and certainly will find no solution apart from a metaphysical hypothesis previously posed at least as a provisional postulate, as is done by algebraists when they wish to solve an equation. Several possible solutions are first proposed hypothetically, and then the equation is solved in terms of these variable values. Our problem, however, is apparently simplified for us since there are evidently only two possible hypotheses. Either the subject is uncreated and therefore participates in the nature of the Absolute—and a theory of knowledge based on this hypothesis is conceivable; or else the subject is created, and in this case we must devise another theory of knowledge of the dialogistic type, the subject being no more solitary or self-contained in the act of thinking than in the act of living or existing. If we are unwilling to accept either hypothesis, we must then imagine a conscious subject in a condition in which nothing could be found in the mind that would justify metaphysical knowledge. Yet this would require a radical separation of the subject from the Absolute, and we would no longer find any means of communication between the subject and the Absolute.

But it will be objected immediately that the question is to know whether there really is any Absolute considered as the cause or source of the subject's origin. In the present stage of our proceedings we do not know this with certainty. How shall we find a way out of the circle?

Other objections will be made against our alternative by those who appeal to the history of philosophy, and especially modern philosophy. There are certain philosophical systems which accept neither the metaphysics of creation nor the hypotheses of Spinoza and Schelling. Not knowing whether beings are created or uncreated, and stating more exactly that they are not created because there is no Absolute and yet for the same reason are not uncreated either, some contemporary philosophies teach that beings exist as a matter of fact but that they possess no metaphysical justification. They are meaningless, and their existence is absurd also. The existence of multiple beings cannot be explained by the metaphysics of creation, they say, nor within a metaphysical hypothesis of the pantheistic type, which at least provides a mythical explanation of the empirical existence emerging from the One. There is in fact no explanation at all.

The choice between the two metaphysical hypotheses which we have indicated can be rejected by a refusal to pursue the metaphysical quest itself, in order to concentrate wholly upon the analysis and description of the empirical data. This is the critical position, and it is also the position of the positivists. Or it can be said that existence is absurd, while refusing to attempt any metaphysical explanation of being. This is a dogmatic position which makes an affirmation instead of suspending judgment concerning the question. It is therefore a position that is neither methodological nor a provisional criticism. It is still a metaphysical thesis. But this metaphysical thesis proceeds from a refusal to undertake the metaphysical inquiry that aims to explain existence. It is a thesis which is based on the Kantian critique, and on positivism and phenomenology. But while the metaphysical affirmation in phenomenology, strictly so called, is merely suspended in a provisional way and for the sake of method, there is a leap of the mind in the philosophies which affirm the absurdity of existence by which they deliberately make the methodological and provisional suspension of the metaphysical inquiry a dogma and propose this suspension on ontological judgment as a definite and final metaphysical position. It is here that the internal contradiction will be found in the contemporary philosophies of the absurd. In any case, we can conclude only one of two things. On the one hand, there must be a suspension of judgment in regard to the metaphysical inquiry either because it is believed that the inquiry is beyond the mind's scope (which is the critical position), or because it seems preferable, for the sake of method, to take cognizance of what is given to us in experience without touching on metaphysical questions, leaving this effort to others (which is the position taken by most scholars today). Or finally it may be supposed that there can be only positive and empirical knowledge (which is the position of positivism, allied with the critical position). However, in the various modalities of this first case, there is a real *suspension* of judgment. There is no attempt to decide anything regarding the Absolute, whether by affirmation or negation. This agnosticism is methodological. It is coherent, valid and useful.

But on the other hand, a suspension of judgment may not seem satisfactory, and it may be decided that there is no

Absolute. In this case, the phenomenological and methodological hypothesis is abandoned, and a metaphysical theory is proposed. It is affirmed that beings exist, but without justification and with no metaphysical ground or cause, or any radical origin in being. This is an inhibition of the spontaneous process of thought which seeks the explanation of existence. There is a deliberate and definitive exclusion of the provisional and methodological omission of the metaphysical inquiry. Phenomenology is changed from methodology into ontology. There is no longer a willingness to describe things as they appear, while provisionally postponing judgment on problems concerning being. It is affirmed that the phenomenon is all there is, and that phenomena have no ontological foundation. The suppression of the thing-in-itself by the post-Kantians did not include a rejection of the Absolute. On the contrary, Fichte, Schelling, Hegel and Schopenhauer established an ontology which based the world of representation upon the absolute Self, or upon the gradually evolving Absolute of the universe, or on the Will. But some contemporary philosophies apparently claim to have rejected the Absolute entirely, while retaining only the phenomenal. For what purpose is this prohibition imposed on human reason, forbidding its connatural efforts to seek the foundation and cause of being? Is this done in the name of the Kantian critique? Kant himself never rejected the thing-in-itself, and if his immediate successors rejected the latter as contradictory per se, they considered the absolute subject as the ground and cause of representation, or rather they though in terms of the Absolute as a subject. Furthermore, it seemed entirely permissible for us to point out that the Kantian critique was not decisive as a justifiable prohibition of the ontological inquiry of human thought. Is positivism the reason for such a prohibition? But positivism is a denial of metaphysics. It could not possibly justify any metaphysical thesis, even if it were negative. Can phenomenology be the excuse? This suspension of judgment, however, this parenthetical omission of metaphysical questions, is methodological and not metaphysical. If it were metaphysical, it would no longer be a methodical suspension of metaphysical judgment. The philosophies of the absurd and the irrational oscillate between the phenomenological and the dogmatic points of view. They dogmatize a methodical doubt.

Absurdity certainly exists, but not in being. It will be found in the movement of the mind which goes successively from a point of view that is phenomenological, as a method, to a point of view that is dogmatic, although these two points of view are contradictory and incompatible. The idea of the absurdity of being or existence, like the idea of nothingness which was so competently analyzed by Bergson, is one of those negative ideas which are actually nothing more than pseudo-concepts, implying contradiction, because they merely express a mental annulment of what has just been stated.

However, if the Kantian critique was not decisive enough to prevent us from proceeding with our metaphysical inquiry, and if Kant's conclusions did not seem to be necessarily inevitable, how is any metaphysical knowledge really possible? We cannot simply reject the Kantian critique, and we shall find no easy solution to the problem.

How is metaphysical knowledge possible? As far as scientific knowledge is concerned, we see with Kant that it exists and can be successfully verified. Therefore it is possible. Under what conditions is it possible? This is a question, once again, which poses and implies metaphysical problems. What is implied in the fact that the mathematician, the physicist and the astrophysicist have knowledge of the universe, and that their calculations actually correspond to verifiable reality, the planets being found exactly where the calculations had said they would be? This whole series of questions requires a special epistemological and metaphysical study.

But what can be said about metaphysical knowledge, that vaunted learning which, as Kant tells us, has been unsuccessful because it has failed to convince? What is this false or true metaphysical knowledge, and how is it possible? Is it merely a kind of optical illusion?

We have mentioned that the problem of metaphysical knowledge could be treated only on the basis of two hypotheses, and we had to go far afield to eliminate the point of view of those who uphold the possibility of a coherent affirmation that being is neither created nor uncreated, but simply meaningless.

We can now return to our alternative. The subject (and the universe as a whole) is either created or uncreated. We can no more say of the conscious subject than of the universe (of which the subject is a component part) that the latter is neither created nor uncreated. We shall consider this point more fully in regard to the universe itself, but insofar as the conscious subject is concerned we must determine how it is possible to know and legitimately infer from the datum of experience to what is not empirically given. We shall see, moreover, that the problem of knowledge is linked to the problem of experience itself, since experience is also something given, and it is precisely this "something given" which must be accounted for.

It is not satisfactory or sufficient to ascertain and observe the datum and say that empirical knowledge is valid simply because it is based upon the experimental datum. The datum itself must be explained. This was clearly realized by a philosopher like Fichte. The empirically given requires explanation, and Fichte attempts this by showing how the datum of our representation proceeds from the self in an unconscious way, so that the conscious subject has the illusion of discovering and perceiving a reality that seems to be extraneous to the self.

This theory of illusion is very ancient, in fact quite as ancient as the metaphysical systems that were apparently unaware of the idea of creation or else simply reject it. In the Upanishads we find the doctrine which tells us that the external world is illusory, being merely a representation or dream of the Absolute, or perhaps even a nightmare! The task is to discover that multiple existence, with its cares and concerns, is only an illusion, for in reality we are truly the Absolute ourselves and to the Absolute we need only return. Plato, in the allegory of the cave, also teaches that the world of our experience is only shadow and reflection. To find the real world again there must be a conversion and a return. Plotinus shows us how the multiple proceeds from the One by a movement that is a descent as well as an illusion. All the monads are the One, but they have forgotten this fact; they have forgotten their Father from whom, however, they have never been really separated although they turned away from Him.

In all these metaphysics, or rather in these various expressions of the same metaphysical tradition, experience is interpreted mythically perhaps, but at least there is some attempt to account for it.

Kant, for his part, answered the question of experience by the famous saying in which he declared that since there is an appearing, there must be something that appears. The post-Kantians rejected this "something," but they explain the genesis of experience and of nature as proceeding from the Absolute, which is the subject.

In all these instances, experience is somehow accounted for, and a metaphysical hypothesis is posed. And when Kant affirms that it is necessary to suppose something that appears, he also becomes metaphysical within the critique itself. His successors have often reproached him for this.

If the subject, like the world of representation, does not originate in the Absolute by creation, if the knowing subject (aware of this or not) is the Absolute, a theory of metaphysical knowledge is wholly possible, as we have already noted. It is even rather easy, for it is by a conversion, the return into oneself, and by a movement which separates us from the external world, liberating us from the temporal, spatial and corporeal that metaphysical knowledge is attained: that is, by a movement which leads us from the exterior to the interior, and from there to the superior. It is intuition. It is a recovery of ourselves in our true nature, which is divine and should never have ceased being so. In fact, it never has ceased to be divine except in our imagination or in our opinion. Actually, I am the Absolute myself, and so are you—so are we all, for we are only One. Metaphysical knowledge is the knowledge of oneself, the knowledge of that Self which is awake and aware beneath the empirical self, lulled and deceived by appearances. Metaphysical knowledge is ascetical, a liberation of the body, a recognition and remembering. It is a gnosis. But there is still something to be explained, a real mystery, which the metaphysical systems of this kind explain very unsatisfactorily.

It is the mystery of the separation between the subject, which is ourselves, and the Absolute. Why must there be any schism between myself and the Absolute that I am? Why is it necessary for the sages of the Veda, or Plotinus or Spinoza, to teach me the truth and the way back to the Absolute that is myself, and which I have ceased to be? Briefly, why must there be the illusion of multiple existence, and what accounts for the ignorance of everyone except a few gnostics? Is there any justification for this fall, this alienation, this dream and exile from the Absolute?

On this point it must be admitted that the metaphysics of this type, from the Upanishads and Plato to Plotinus, Spinoza, Fichte, Schelling and Hegel, all answer us with myths that are doubtless admirable. But nothing could ever compel us to accept the beautiful and terrible tale of the fall of souls and the alienation from the divine Substance. We might accept it voluntarily, perhaps—but then, as was said before, we would no longer be pursuing our metaphysical inquiry nor would our endeavor be serious or scientific any more, for this would be an imaginary evasion of the problem. This might be legitimate, of course, but it would not be convincing to human reason.

If we continue our investigation of the problem of knowledge by adopting now the contrary point of view of the metaphysics of creation—although still only as an hypothesis—the whole problem of knowledge will be posed in a different way. The empirical reality is given, but not by the self as the conscious subject. It is given independently of the conscious subject (which is the self) and independently of all *created* conscious subjects, but this does not mean that it is given independently of any conscious subject whatsoever. The hypothesis of an uncreated conscious subject—the Creator—still remains. Empirical reality now has a completely different consistency from that in the metaphysics of the Upanishads or even in Plato and Plotinus. It is created, and this means that it is not illusory. No change or conversion of cognition or knowledge can dispel it like a bad dream. Time and space do not measure a fall or an alienation, but rather a position and a beginning.

By turning inward to ourselves, or by an awakening, we shall not find the Absolute within us, for we are not the Absolute. According to this hypothesis, the Absolute is *other* than ourselves. We must go out of ourselves to know this Other.

However, if the Absolute is the Other, in relation to ourselves, it does not necessarily mean that the Absolute is therefore *distant* from us spatially. In fact, if we are created beings, it means that we are sustained and quickened by this Creator. The problem of our existing, acting and thinking is no longer posed in solitary terms, but rather as a dialogue, dialectically. We are created beings and we are ourselves, but we are not so in any self-sufficient way. We act, but we are not the creators of the energy by which we act, nor of the arm which we raise, nor of the organism which we constitute. We think, but the thought which is our own seems to come from a source that is indeed within ourselves, but which we have not created either. We have already noted that things certainly do present themselves in this way to our consciousness and our reflective thought, in our immediate experience.

Metaphysical systems that reject the idea of creation will protest that it is precisely this immediate datum of our reflective consciousness which is an illusion. Morever, it is this feeling that the external world exists independently of our unconscious power which is quite illusory. Likewise, our impression that we receive existence and the power to think and act from an Other is an illusion also. It is this illusion which must be dispelled by an awareness and acknowledgment that we, in fact, are the Creator of ourselves and of the world as well.

But these metaphysical systems urge us to make the acknowledgment of our own divine essence on the basis of myths, by telling us the tragic epic of the fall or alienation of souls from the Absolute, which really means a self-exile and alienation of the Absolute. They ask us to reject the immediate and apparently certain datum of our reflective consciousness, and to accept a tale which itself is much less immediate and much less certain. The intuition which they invite us to exercise by a conversion that will dispel the illusion of multiple and individual existence will then steep us in a sentiment or assurance of absoluteness. But why should we put more trust in this ecstatic experience than in the common experience of common sense? The metaphysics of creation can also point to mystics who tell about an ecstatic experience, not in terms of a return to the One but rather as a loving dialogue with an *Other*.

At the level of metaphysical reflection we see no decisive reason for abandoning the immediate and substantial experience of what is empirically given, whether it be the external world or this something *given* which we are to ourselves, merely to put our trust in an experience that rejects this datum and repudiates it.

We must realize that we are now confronting a definite choice which has to be made although we have no external criterion to help us decide. We can choose between an intellectual speculation whose point of departure is the common empirical datum, and a metaphysical point of view that repudiates this common experience, preferring another kind of experience which is ecstatic. There is no third perspective, serving as a criterion external to both, from which we might be able to choose between the two. We are obliged to use whatever is at our disposal in making this choice, including reflective thought, of course, but the whole of our being also. In man, thought must not be dissociated from being and doing, for this leads him to derangement. Madness can be quite accurately defined as a mind dissociated from being and doing, a mind which, in man, would constitute a world apart, a kind of thinking that is exclusively mental.

Once again we confront something *given* (an experience which we did not originate, neither consciously nor unconsciously) with our common sense and with a mind whose cognitive powers must be used as fully as possible, a reason whose demands become increasingly more explicit, according as human thought—and especially scientific thought—is formed and advances. But we are not the creators of reason, which is the exigence of coherent thought in a thinking subject who is not uncreated, and is not his own creator.

In these circumstances, how will metaphysical knowledge be

justifiable? Apparently we are turning round and round within a circle, indefinitely, and we find ourselves enclosed—but as a matter of fact we are progressively probing a situation that is the condition of all mankind.

We accept our existence and carry on our life and activity, spending the energy within us without posing this critical question, or if we do wonder about it for a passing moment we quickly dismiss it and get on with our daily business. The heart continues to beat within us without any consent of our will, and we have no say in the matter. Strictly speaking, of course, we can stop its beating, but we are unable *to give life to ourselves.* We are alive, and this is sufficient for us. We enjoy living, but we do not create the life within us.

Science, for its part, periodically poses the question of how scientific knowledge is possible, and how the mind of man attains to its grasp and understanding of the structure of the world and of matter: even foreseeing the existence of an unknown planet, or an atom which has not yet been verified empirically, or a fossil not yet unearthed. But the scientist continues his fruitful work of research and gathers the harvest although he may never be able to answer this question. He may ponder it, but his failure to find an answer does not prevent the continuing of his labor for science. Man goes on living, acting, moving about, and perceiving the world, although he has not solved the problem of the ground and cause of his existence, the source of energy for his activity, or the possibility of knowledge. However, he makes an act of faith in life and in his own knowledge. And this act of faith works wonders for him.

In metaphysical matters man is less easily convinced, because while science makes its discovery of the planet which was foretold, and the fossil that is required, actually verifying its hypotheses empirically, metaphysics, on the other hand, has no instrument of empirical verification. It is a quest that leads us into a void, so to speak, far beyond the verifiable. We have only an inner criterion to guide us, the criterion of the strict logical cogency of our proceedings. However, Kant has shown quite precisely that this logical cogency in rational proceedings does not exclude the possibility of illusion. He tells us that reason's venture, outside of experience, has no object at all.

We all readily make an act of faith in order to continue living, without knowing how or why, or to raise an arm even though we are not the source of the energy we use, and do not even know the way that all this occurs. We also make it for the purpose of continuing experimental science although we are unable to explain the correspondence of the mind and reality. But it is an act which we refuse to make with regard to metaphysical inquiry because the latter is apparently unsuccessful (since there is plurality and antinomy in metaphysics) and we possess no means whatever to verify any metaphysical assertion experimentally.

Quite obviously, we do not have any means of verifying a metaphysical assertion *experimentally*, because the order which metaphysics claims to explore does not lie within the field that is observed and tested by experimental instruments. We cannot verify the existence of the Absolute, or its non-existence. It is possible neither immediately nor mediately, by means of instruments, nor through our visual, tactile or olfactory senses, nor with a scale or microscope. Our senses make contact with experimental reality directly, or mediately through instruments that simply serve to increase our own capacities. Our senses are the organs of experience. But the metaphysical quest consists precisely in seeking to know what is implicit and supposed in experience and in reality as a whole. This process is not itself sensible, for there is nothing to be seen or touched. It is wholly an intellectual process and effort, taking as its point of departure the empirical and sensible datum. However, as a process, it is neither empirical nor verifiable by the means and instruments of experimental science. Its validity is entirely dependent on its own intrinsic coherence and logical cogency. If it is said that no object corresponds to our metaphysical reflection, the statement must be proved—and in our opinion Kant does not seem to have offered this necessary proof. He bases his critical analysis on a presupposition which is precisely in question, i.e., the subject does not find within himself the necessary resources for transcending what is empirically given, because it is taken for granted that he is in circumstances of a limiting kind. But these same circumstances or limitations would make it impossible for him to justify or account for scientific knowledge, or even the most elementary cognition, or his activity, his living or existence.

To be consistent, the mind's act of faith in itself, which is refused whenever it is a question of metaphysical research, should also be refused when the mind ventures into the field of science, and even when it concerns man's very act of living, considered as his willingness to live and to act. It serves no purpose at all to say that science has a verifiable object, and therefore empirical knowledge is valid simply because its method is successful, while metaphysical inquiry has no object, since it has ended in failure as its antinomies prove. The historical antinomies of human reason are matters of fact, but they prove nothing per se. Metaphysics may not have succeeded until now—perhaps even in nothing at all—but this does not prove that success is impossible in the future. In any case, nobody has the right to say that metaphysics is without a real object, for this is exactly what remains to be seen. If no experience of the senses can confirm the existence of the object of metaphysical reflection, an experience of another kind might be able to do so.

We realize, of course, that this could lead us away from the order of metaphysical reflection, and for that reason we will not consider an abandonment of this purely rational procedure in order to venture forth into the order of mysticism. It is, however, paralogistic to say that the object of metaphysical reflection does not exist simply because it does not come within the scope of our empirical knowledge, since as a matter of fact the object of metaphysical reflection is not itself perceptible, but is the ground and cause of the perceptible. It is another paralogism to insist that metaphysical reflection has no object because transcendental analysis claims to have proved that the conscious subject is incapable of propounding a truth that cannot be empirically confirmed. This is dogmatizing about the nature of the conscious subject, without any metaphysical justification for the interdict, and it would indeed be difficult to provide such justification, since metaphysical reflection is suspended as long as the subject's capacity for metaphysical knowledge remains unconfirmed.

It seems, in fact, that there really is an inner criterion of validity for the process of metaphysical reflection. This criterion is the logical cogency and the coherence of the proceedings. But the criterion of logic does not prove that thought, in its metaphysical proceedings, arrives at any real object. The intrinsic logic of a metaphysical inquiry is not sufficient proof that the endeavor has culminated in the attainment of ontological truth. The real criterion of the value of metaphysical inquiry is not found in the conscious subject who must verify the logical coherence of his proceedings every step of the way, but can do no more than this. The definitive and ultimate criterion of the validity of metaphysical reflection is found in the object of cognition, the reality attained, and in the being that is known, which is the Absolute, if the Absolute exists. Here again, we ascertain what was declared at the start of this study: the criterion of rationality is to be found in reality. Whatever exists is rational. Whatever does not exist is irrational, fictitious and mythical.

If there be any criterion, in the sense of an inner touchstone of logic, it is not really a sufficient criterion, for in its turn it must be verified by the result achieved, that is to say, by the reality that is known. If the endeavor is apparently logical but fails to attain to anything real, we can no longer say that the proceedings were logical. Whatever exists is true, and if metaphysical reflection seeks to discover the Absolute, the whole endeavor will be cogent, logical and true if the Absolute exists. It will be illusory, as Kant declares, if it has not attained to knowledge of the Absolute, but rather to some chimerical fabrication of its own. According to Kant, this would not prove that the Absolute does not exist, but only that this is beyond the scope of rational knowledge. The exigencies of practical reason might lead us to the Absolute, but metaphysical reflection, as Kant repeats insistently, cannot go beyond itself. It cannot attain to the Absolute even though the Absolute exists.

Kant made a critical study of the historic proofs for the existence of God, and doubtless this was quite valid in regard to the proofs that Kant examined. However, it is questionable whether the Kantian critique is relevant to the metaphysical studies of St. Thomas, St. Anselm or Descartes. We need not enter into this historic controversy now. The metaphysical quest which culminates in the discernment of the Absolute as the foundation of reality is valid if there really is an Absolute attained by this endeavor. It is futile and illusory if no Absolute exists, or at least if what is apparently attained under the impression of discovering the Absolute is not really the Absolute at all.

In brief, truth is the criterion of rationality. The ultimate criterion is not found in the proceedings of reason, although there are inner criteria of logic and coherence. The ultimate and absolute criterion is found in the object and terminus of the proceedings, in whatever has been attained. It is imprudent in science to pre-determine what is rational and what is not—as science itself has taught us—the criterion of rationality being found in reality alone, for what at first may seem irrational finally wins acceptance because of its existence. So likewise in metaphysical matters and proceedings we cannot undertake a purely internal critique of knowledge unless we make allowance for what is known and true. Neither knowledge nor reason can be dissociated from truth. The Kantian critique is based upon a factitious presupposition, an uncritical and artificial separation between the conscious subject and being. Inevitably and ultimately, the mind no longer finds anything within itself which would confirm its consciousness of existence. The subject remains enclosed in a total subjectivity, simply because of an analysis conducted in artificial circumstances and conditions that are not relevant to the subject at all.

Metaphysical inquiry will therefore require our constant surveillance and unceasing critical reflection with regard to the process itself, but we cannot undertake a critique of the power of cognition prior to this inquiry. At best it will have to follow upon the success of the inquiry, and be retrospective. We shall have to put our trust in the coherence of our thinking, just as the scientist does, and as all living men do. We shall be obliged to make use of the gift of thought as we avail ourselves of life and motion, although we are not the authors of them. But this gift must be used humbly, with a metaphysical humility, which is simply the clear awareness of our condition as creatures. We must make use of the mind although we did not create it and do not have absolute possession of the secret, nor integral knowledge of the power, of our human thought processes. We shall have to use the processes of thought in such a way that we avail ourselves of everything in the world that is *given*. The verification of the absolute truth we are seeking will not be provided by the process itself, but only by the Being that is attained by our endeavor, just as in science the calculation, no matter how exact it may be, requires objective experimental verification. But in metaphysics the objective verification is not perceptible, and the experience, if there be any experience, is neither tangible nor visible.

We make use of reason as an instrument, although we do not know how the validity of the instrument is guaranteed, but the criterion of validity which can guarantee the value and usefulness of our reason can only be found in the absolute ground and cause of rationality. In practice, rationalism makes confident use of reason as the only guide available to us, just as it puts trust in the empirically given. The rationalism of contemporary science does not raise the question of the ground and criterion of rationality. It uses reason with strict precision, as something *given*, and it is right in doing so.

However, if we seek the criterion and ground of rationality, they can be found only at the ontological level, and if we want reason's worth to be verified before we reach this ontological and absolute level that justifies reason's exercise we shall obviously find no inner criterion which could justify a *metaphysical* use of reason.

Clearly stated, we may say that the use of reason in metaphysical inquiry and method is justified within a theological perspective, and rationalism is justifiable from this same perspective. But if we want to justify the use of reason at the metaphysical level without basing this justification on God, we will no longer find any criterion of validity. And the critique is right in refusing to accept the proof of God's existence as long as the metaphysical use of reason remains unjustified. In this case, however, the metaphysical use of reason would no longer be defensible, because it can only be justified from an ontological and theological point of view.

Finally, all of this proves that we will not find anything in the intrinsic examination of the use of reason which would justify reason's worth and usefulness. The exercise of rationality is something given, which serves our purposes with more or less precision but which can ultimately be justified only by the absolute truth in which it originates and to which it sometimes attains.

Until this truth is attained, which justifies and sustains reason's proceedings, there can be no absolute justification of reason, any more than of existence or life. Until truth is discovered, human reason, like our life itself, can only put its trust in its own activity, its own requirements, and its own aspirations.

Let us briefly recapitulate the results which have now been apparently established by this long and difficult analysis.

We must not suppose that there are any number of possible metaphysical hypotheses.

Either reality is based upon the Absolute or established within the Absolute, but the relation between the Absolute and empirical reality is not one of creation. Empirical reality, the world itself, is the Absolute, or a modality or part of absolute substance, but alienated and exiled. According to this hypothesis, a theory of knowledge is possible. The human conscious subject is a portion of the divine substance. The Absolute can be known by a "conversion" which releases the subject from the illusion of individual existence. He will discover that he is a part of the Divine Mind, and that his own nature is divine. He will return to that anterior Unity which individual existence made him forsake, at least apparently. He will be wholly immersed in the Absolute, the source of his being. Metaphysical knowledge, in this hypothesis, is a gnosis, a transcending insight by which the human soul discovers simultaneously its real identity and source, and the heights from which it has fallen. It is by this discovery of its origin and nature that it now returns to the Absolute that has always been the soul's true Self, although this had been forgotten.

This metaphysical hypothesis is one possibility. As a matter of fact, this is the metaphysics which has widely prevailed in a long tradition extending from the Upanishads to Plotinus, Spinoza, Fichte, Schelling and Hegel.

If we do not accept this pantheistic kind of metaphysics which rejects or is unaware of the idea of a creation we can turn toward a metaphysics which also affirms that the world has an absolute ground and cause, considered however as both transcendent and immanent. In a metaphysics of creation, as found in the Hebrew and Christian tradition, the world is indeed established within the Absolute, and finds its sufficient cause in the Absolute. But the world does not emanate from the Absolute in the manner and mode suggested by the Upanishads, Plotinus, Spinoza, or Hegel. The world does not originate in the Absolute by necessity, but freely. The world is neither a modality nor an emanation of absolute substance. The human soul is not a portion of the divine substance. Empirical reality is *created* by the Absolute conceived as transcendent and free.

In this metaphysical system, which is the metaphysics of orthodox Judaism and Christianity, the problem of knowledge is posed, and can also be approached, with some hope of solution. It is posed even more than in Hindu or Neoplatonic metaphysics, because we are not portions of the absolute substance, and to know the Absolute something more is required than a return to our pre-existent condition. In Jewish and Christian metaphysics the Absolute is wholly other than ourselves, and we are onto-logically distinct from the Absolute. The differentiation and distinction between beings is not an illusion which a transformed understanding dispels, but a reality arising from creation itself. The relationship between the human conscious subject and the Absolute is not ultimately a relationship of identity—as the Upanishads affirm by saying: thou art the Absolute—but rather a dialogistic relationship between Myself and Thee, as Martin Buber has pointed out.

There really is a problem of knowledge, because of the existence of beings *other* than the human conscious subject. But the problem of knowledge can be reflectively considered and perhaps even solved.

Finally, it can be maintained, and it has been maintained, that objective empirical reality rests upon no Absolute whatsover. There simply is no Absolute. Objective reality has no sufficient cause. It is irrational and meaningless. In this hypothesis there is no longer any metaphysical problem of knowledge of the Absolute, since the Absolute is radically denied.

But an hypothesis of this kind itself requires a rational support and basis. The affirmation is not sufficient from the philosophical point of view, which we have taken. We want to know the reasons. And these reasons are especially needed because in the hypothesis of an irrational world we must repress a natural and spontaneous tendency of our thinking, which cannot be satisfied with the simple ascertainment of the fact of the world's existence, and inevitably seeks the rational basis of this existence. To affirm that the world is irrational, and without any ground or cause—or without a sufficient reason, as Leibnitz called it—is an important thesis which requires proof.

It is not possible to take refuge behind the Kantian critique in hope of proving that there is no absolute ontological basis for empirical reality, because it is precisely this critique itself which must account for its own position among these three possible metaphysical positions.

However, the Kantian critique is incompatible with any of the three hypotheses. Some will say that the critique is right in this respect because it cannot presuppose the truth of any metaphysics before deciding whether or not the human mind possesses the ability to undertake metaphysical study. The Kantian critique therefore refrains from making any metaphysical presupposition, and with good reason.

Nevertheless, the question once again is to know whether the problem of knowledge can be treated, and more especially if it can be resolved, without reference to any metaphysical position. *The Kantian conscious subject is without a metaphysical status.*

Apparently we are trapped within a vicious circle. There can be no legitimate metaphysics without a critique of knowledge.

There is no valid critique of knowledge without metaphysics, which gives a metaphysical status, at least hypothetically, to the conscious subject under consideration.

Perhaps it would be more correct to follow the example of mathematicians who pose an hypothesis, and then examine the results in relation to the problem that was propounded. Another hypothesis is then tried, and the process continues for all possible hypotheses.

Kant places the conscious subject outside of every metaphysical hypothesis. Set forth in this way, the problem of knowledge has, of course, no solution. All that Kant has proved is that in the terms in which he poses this problem of knowledge, it is a a problem that cannot be solved. He has proved this point, but nothing more. If we do not suppose that the conscious subject depends on or originates in the Absolute in some way, we will never find anything in the reflective analysis of the conscious subject's cognitive processes that would justify metaphysical knowledge. The conscious subject, alone, possesses nothing per se, or interiorly, that could possibly account for the act of metaphysical knowledge. This is what is proved by Kant's critique. But no one ever doubted it. It is simply a question of knowing whether the human conscious subject is in fact alone, or is fundamentally established in the Absolute, either in the way suggested by Plotinus, Spinoza or Schelling, or in the manner proposed by the Jewish and Christian metaphysics of creation.

The problem of knowledge has no solution unless an ontological status is given to the conscious subject. If we consider the conscious subject alone, wholly subjective and with no ontological foundation, the problem of knowledge is without any possible answer. And if we are unwilling to consider the metaphysical problem of the conscious subject's ontological status before determining the subject's capacity for metaphysical knowledge (considering the subject in isolation), we are indeed enclosed within a circle. What shall we do to break out of this circle?

In our human circumstances the problem of knowledge is unlikely to receive a fully satisfactory solution *before* the Absolute is attained. In view of the discursive condition of our thinking,

our speculations are not in fact fully verified as long as absolute
truth remains unattained.

It does not seem likely that Kant's critique can inhibit the
proceedings of metaphysical thought, because his analysis is
undertaken with factitious presuppositions as the point of departure.

Metaphysical thought can still do what is done by scientific
thought: move forward while putting its trust in human reason
and regarding it as reliable, simply because human reason is our
only resource. The act of knowing cannot be completely accounted for at the start any more than the beating of the heart
or the very act of walking. But it is important to realize that we
cannot fully account for our existence or life, or knowledge,
before we understand the metaphysical ground and cause. Human
reason has nothing in itself that could account for its own proceedings. But the condition of human reason in this respect is no
different from that of the universe as a whole.

Both the universe and ourselves within it appear before us
as something given, which we did not create, nor did it create
itself.

It is this realization that nothing is self-created (applied to
the universe as a whole) that constitutes our awareness of
radical insufficiency in regard to existence generally, the universe
as a whole, and also that element of the universe which we are.
The universe, like ourselves, is unable to account for its own
existence. It exists, as a matter of fact, but this is a fact for
which there is no inherent explanation. If the objection is made
that no ontological justification is necessary, and we need only
ascertain the fact, we can reply by pointing out that this would
be a renunciation of the exercise of intelligence in its metaphysical
speculations. The point of view of positivism must then be
adopted, together with a refusal to satisfy the demand for complete intelligibility, which is inscribed in human reason. The level
of metaphysical reflection would consequently be abandoned.
We need not follow the objector, therefore, in this direction.

This radical insufficiency of the whole visible universe, and
of all that it contains, to account for its existence becomes ap-

parent first of all from the perspective of existence. The universe is there before us, with all the beings which exist within it. Not one of them was self-created. And the totality of beings and realities which constitute the universe was not self-created either. The universe is not uncreated, however, nor are any of the beings that inhabit and constitute it. Everything in the universe appeared at a particular moment in time, and everything it comprises, let us add, is perishable. Everything in the universe has been *born*, and the totality of beings and realities which constitute the universe is subject to this universal law of birth, quite as inevitably as each reality in particular. The universe is not the Absolute, and nothing in the universe, no particular element whatsoever, is the Absolute.

This postulate, which is an immediate datum of positive experience, is contradicted by the metaphysics which teaches the divinity of the universe. This can be done either ingenuously as the Greeks did, or in a more abstruse way, as is done by several philosophical systems which do not teach that the cosmos is a divine animal, as the Stoics maintained, or a sentient god, as Plato declared. Instead they propose a theory that considers the world to be a modality of divine substance, an aspect of the Absolute, and regards nature as an alienation of the Absolute, or some other mode of relationship between the world and the Absolute, excluding creation. These metaphysical systems which teach that the world, nature, matter and multiplicity constitute the alienated Absolute, or a modality of the Absolute, regard the multiple world of our representation as illusory, as we have already noted. A transformed consciousness discerns the Absolute beneath the multiplicity of beings dispersed through space and time. Man himself, as we saw, is a portion of divine substance. It is simply a matter of discovering the truth about the world and nature once again, and this truth is the Absolute, self-conscious at last, and no longer alienated. A metaphysics of this type tends to disparage the world and empirical reality to the advantage of an insight which discerns the One beneath the multiple. It is idealistic.

We can approach this kind of metaphysics from another

angle—from the reverse side, so to speak. Now it will not teach that the world is the Absolute in alienation, or that it should be considered as one of the modalities of the Absolute, and that the appearances of matter and multiplicity are dispelled in the initiated contemplation of the gnostic. Now it is affirmed that the Absolute is indeed the world, but the doctrine of a transformed consciousness which makes materiality disappear should be rejected. Instead of the pantheistic idealism which teaches the divinity of the Universe considered as a representation or a modality or alienation of the Absolute, we now confront a materialism which confers all the predicates of the Absolute upon the universe and matter generally, including aseity, eternity and infinity. The metaphysics of the Upanishads, Spinoza or Hegel is exchanged for the metaphysics of Marx and Engels. However, both of these metaphysical systems have the same point of departure. Both teach that the universe is uncreated, but idealism proposes the doctrine of an alienation and a fall, while the materialism of Marx and Engels justly considers this doctrine as both mythical and phantasmagorical.

Marx and Engels began with the presuppositions of German idealism, but they rejected the doctrine of the alienation and gradual evolution of the Absolute. They borrowed the idea of alienation from metaphysics or mythology and transferred it to political and economic matters. But they held fast to the fundamental postulate of German idealism and of Spinoza's philosophy, affirming that the universe is uncreated. The idea of creation, according to Marx, and in the opinion of Spinoza and Fichte, is *"the absolute fundamental error"* (Fichte, *Initiation à la vie bienheureuse*, 6th lecture). Marx wants to rid the mind of the people of this idea of creation. He admits that it is a conception which will be very difficult to remove from common consciousness *(Nationalökonomie und Philosophie*, X, pagination of Marx). But both nature and man must be considered as self-existent, that is to say, *durchsichselbstsein.* This is the doctrine of aseity applied to nature and to man.

A being is self-sufficient, as Marx tells us, if the self alone is the source of existence, but a being whose life is willed by another being, is in a dependent condition. If my own life was

created by an Other, and I am only alive because of His will,
I am dependent on Him. It is an Other who is the *source* of my
life, and my life would thus have its ground and cause outside of
itself if it is not my own creation. Marx adds that the concept
of creation is difficult to extirpate because the idea of the self-
sufficiency and aseity of nature and man is contrary to all the
habits of practical life. Doubtless, Marx means that man's propensity for making things (i.e., man's *praxis*) somehow produces
the illusion that the universe is also something made, as the
watch is made by the watchmaker. Marx therefore criticizes the
idea of creation by a dialectical method (which Bergson was to
use in his criticism of other ideas), maintaining that *homo faber*
transposes to the level of speculation habits of thought which are
only valid with regard to the making of things.

To this affirmation of the aseity of nature and man, Marx
adds a remarkable paralogism, telling us that the idea of the
creation of the earth, and more generally of the universe, has
received a fatal blow from our scientific knowledge of the evolution of the earth and the universe which, according to Marx,
clearly reveals the process of the earth's evolution as a self-
creation (*Selbsterzeugung*). But this statement is entirely paralogistic, for the science of the world's becoming, or the evolution
of the universe and of matter or life, in no way implies that this
evolution is self-sufficient or self-creative. In reading Marx or
Engels, we find many passages affirming this ontological self-
sufficiency of the universe and man, but we can hardly find any
that lift us from the level of impassioned allegations to the heights
of rational discussion. Engels, in the *Dialectics of Nature*, also
teaches the aseity of nature and matter, an eternity of matter
which, in his opinion, moves in an eternal cycle. The elementary
matter of the solar systems, writes Engels, was naturally produced by transformations of motion which are by nature inherent
in moving matter. It is this matter itself which produces both
life and consciousness. In short, matter and motion are provided
with the predicates traditionally attributed to the Absolute:
aseity, eternity, infinity, and creative power. It remains to be
seen whether these propositions are meaningful or not.

It is easy to understand the motives which inspire such

protests and declarations in favor of man's aseity and ontological self-sufficiency. Apart from historic political situations, an adulterated version of the theology of creation was effective in teaching that man's creation was humiliating, degrading and enslaving in its consequences. It is a part of our task to determine how an authentic Christian doctrine of creation, taken from the Bible and the early Fathers of the Church, answers to a certain legitimate desire to save man from "religious alienation," so to speak. The biblical and patristic doctrine of creation does not seek to overwhelm man, or to reduce him to the ignominious condition of a dependent slave, but rather to divinize him. This is the doctrine of *theiôsis*.

At the present stage of our analysis, we are not primarily trying to discover whether man's condition is satisfactory or humiliating, but only to determine what man's condition really is. No matter how we approach or consider the question, it seems difficult, in our opinion, to affirm with Marx that man owes his existence to himself alone and is therefore self-created. We can readily agree with Marxism when it teaches that man's duty is to cooperate in his own creation. In this sense, man really does become the creator of himself, but he begins with something *given*, which is his own existence. Elsewhere in this essay, we shall again consider the matter of man's cooperation in the work of his creation. But concerning this particular point, Marxism touches on something of capital importance, and since it is an idea that is fully traditional in Revelation and in apostolic and patristic thought, we shall find it relatively easy to accept this Marxist insight and requirement. Man appropriates his own existence to himself, as a gift of being, and of energy for action, cooperating in his own genesis and destiny in order that he may grow into the very image and likeness of his Creator, in response to his high calling.

However, at the empirical and elementary level, which concerns us now, the first fact that must be acknowledged is that man is not self-created in his original and empirical existence. This same fact may be affirmed in regard to the universe as a whole.

We cannot, therefore, accept the thesis of those metaphysical systems which divinize the universe explicitly, as was done by the ancient Greek philosophers. All of our positive, empirical, scientific knowledge is opposed to this worship of the cosmos. We know that the stars are not gods; neither is the sun or the moon. Aristotle thought it was proper to place the study of the stars under the heading of theology, and said that the stars are uncreated substances, imperishable and eternal. Plato and the Stoics believed that the universe is a divine animal. But we have brought the universe to a lower status, for we know that nothing within it is divine, nothing can account for its own existence, and nothing has created itself. Nor is the universe as a whole to be considered as a god, any more than the elements which constitute it. There is no longer a divinized or mystifying universe around us today, but rather a universe composed of matter, purely physical, although it is sometimes a living and conscious matter, which is something *given*. We shall soon prove that the lyricism of Engels is quite inappropriate, and always will be in any scientific thinking. Matter is not creative. It cannot account for its own existence nor for the syntheses that are constructed with matter.

Pantheism in all its forms, whether explicit or unavowed as in the case of Marxism, is definitely a mythical metaphysics repudiated by all rational thought which values scientific experience. A choice must be made between the pantheistic myth and rational thought which is supported by scientific verification. One may prefer the position of agnosticism, of course, and simply suspend any judgment concerning the possibility of a metaphysical interpretation of what is empirically given in the cosmos. This is a coherent position, although in our opinion it does not exhaust all the potentialities of human intelligence. But one cannot be a pantheist and still maintain that such thinking can lead to solid convictions by a strictly rational method. No doubt there are many scholars and scientists who profess belief in pantheism, but they have chosen the metaphysics of the eternal cycle and essential divinity of the universe not because of the requirements of reason, but simply as a religious choice. There is a sharp division within the minds of these men, like double-entry bookkeeping, with their scientific, rational thinking in one column, and in the other their preference for a myth. It appears, therefore, that the universe is a reality, a vast ensemble of realities and beings which are not self-created, possessing nothing within themselves that could account for their existence. And the pantheistic hypothesis has not seemed worthy of our acceptance.

However, in the light of all the evidence, although we can no longer suppose that the universe is divine or believe that it is the Absolute since it did not create itself, may we legitimately infer that it has been created by another Being? Obviously, it is not self-created. Nor is it a god or the Absolute. But could it not be said, perhaps, that it is nevertheless uncreated? In other words, between the hypothesis of the divinity of the universe which would justify its eternity along with its existence, and the hypothesis of a creation of the universe, is there no place for an intermediate hypothesis, accepting neither creation nor divinization, but suggesting instead an eternally existing and uncreated universe?

Actually, this intermediate position between pantheism and the metaphysics of creation has but rarely been affirmed in the history of human thought, so far as we know. Metaphysical systems that were unaware of the creation idea, or rejected it, always taught that the universe is a god, or a modality of divine substance. Aseity was explained by divinity. The universe, in fact, was never deemed to be a reality, or an ensemble of realities, which had no Creator and yet was not the Absolute either. This third hypothesis is the one we encountered when we were considering the problem of the conscious subject over and over again. The existence of beings was proposed as something inexplicable, with no absolute ground or cause, and therefore simply meaningless. But the problem of the existence of the universe as a whole is apparently not considered in philosophies of the irrational. These philosophies are of literary inspiration, and cosmological reflection is not their strong point. We may say, therefore, that the hypothesis of the existence of the universe, independently of any Absolute, has had but little acceptance in the history of philosophy, even though an hypothesis of this kind would easily rejoin the hypothesis proposed by philosophies of the irrational and the absurd in regard to beings in the world.

This would be an existence based upon no Absolute whatsoever, neither by emanation nor by alienation, and not by creation: an existence that is inexplicable from the perspective of reason which seeks the ground and cause. It should be kept in mind that a philosophy of this type is based upon a phenomenology that has been given the status of ontology. But phenomenology, as we said before, is a method—wholly legitimate—which cannot substitute for ontology or be transformed into it without some metaphysical justification, and the latter is directly dependent on a process which transcends phenomenological analysis. Consequently, as was previously indicated, we have before us the definite choice to make between a metaphysics of the pantheistic type and the metaphysics of creation. The third hypothesis is not really a metaphysical hypothesis at all, but rather a rejection of metaphysical thought, or else an oscillation between this rejection of ontological thought and the phenomenological method, the latter being considered surreptitiously as an ontology, although it is not one.

In any case, we shall not claim a victory for our own point of view by a simple conclusion that since the pantheistic hypothesis is excessively involved in mythological hypotheses that are challenged by actual experience, there is consequently nothing but the hypothesis of creation to be considered now.

As a matter of fact, the history of metaphysics has alternated between these two poles, and apparently there is no other possibility. However, we have not reached the end of our analyses. It is only after a long consideration of the problem, in all its aspects, that the facts will perhaps become entirely clear to us.

We have stated, as an established fact, that the universe as a whole, and all that it includes, is unable to account for its existence. It is not self-created, but it is there before us, and it evolves progressively; self-constitutive, but it is not the Absolute.

This is a point of view from the aspect of existence in which the universe is regarded as an object, a totality of beings, although not one of them is sufficient to account for its own existence. The whole is no more capable of this than any of its parts.

However, the aspect of existence is not the only one. There is also the aspect of gradual evolution. The universe is not merely an object before us, of which we are a part. The universe is developing. There is a process of creation and evolution.

Finally, there is a third aspect. The universe is infinitely structured. In its diversity it is composed of a vast number of things and beings.

We may consider the universe from the perspective of existence, or in the light of its development and evolution. Or we can study the universe with regard to its structure, attributes and differentiation. All of these aspects, however, need explanation. Not only must we account for the universe simply as something that exists, but also in terms of a process, development and diversification. We must explain its structure, characteristics and nature. The existence of the universe, and its essence and evolution, require an ontological explanation.

The universe did not emerge from nothingness or come forth from the Absolute in its present stage of development. The positive sciences have taught us that it was gradually formed by an evolutionary process that is still continuing. Our planet has not always been inhabited, nor has life always covered raw, physical matter with its thin veneer, as a kind of excrescence. Living matter is the fruit of a long process, the culmination of a synthesis that took millions of years to achieve. Matter itself was not suddenly given its present state, for there has also been an evolution and a compounding of matter. The universe, as we know it today, has already reached an advanced stage of its evolution. It is therefore chimerical to *imagine* that the universe emerged from the Absolute or from nothingness exactly as it appears to us now. The universe was originally much simpler, as far as its material structure is concerned.

Everything within the universe came into being at some

particular moment in time. Matter, at a certain level of complexity, is the result of an evolutionary process which culminated in its appearance at some definite period. Life, or living matter, appeared about one or two billion years ago. Furthermore, all living beings are born and they die. The universe cannot therefore be something static, simply existing—nor even a static ensemble of facts and things. The universe is an evolutionary process in which matter originates, and is transformed and diversified. It becomes particularized in corpuscles that are living, and then conscious, appearing and disappearing. In the course of time, matter develops into forms that are increasingly complex and varied.

Consequently, we shall have to account for the universe not only with regard to its existence, but also with reference to its motion and development, the process of evolution which points toward forms that are more and more complex and complete. It is not merely the existence of the universe that requires explanation, but even more specifically its evolution.

This evolution is defined as a gradual synthesis. Matter becomes increasingly complex in the course of time, which means that syntheses which are more and more astronomically intricate are progressively constituted as time passes. It is this continuous synthesis which we must explain.

The multiple is not sufficient to account for the syntheses in which it is integrated. Let us begin with the most elementary particles. Even their existence must be explained, of course. But let us assume that they are something *given*. From a metaphysical point of view we shall have to account for the synthesis in which the elementary corpuscles are going to be combined and integrated. The particles themselves are not an adequate explanation of the synthesis in which they are incorporated to form a new structural unity. The corpuscles do not suffice to explain the atomic structure in which they are integrated in a highly diversified and complex way. We know, of course, that the problem of synthesis and structure at the micro-physical level is not posed in the same terms as when it concerns the molecular level, for in regard to the former we are not dealing with corpuscles as elements which existed prior to their integration within the cosmic structure that we call the atom. We would be falling back upon the physics of Democritus if we were to pose the problems of the multiple and of its synthesis as though the elementary corpuscles pre-existed apart from their formation within the atomic system. Nevertheless, this structure itself is a system, highly complex. And the system requires explanation. For analytical purposes, at least abstractly, we can distinguish this structure from the elements which it informs. Properly speaking, there is a synthesis of previously existing separate elements at the molecular level.

Atoms cannot provide a satisfactory explanation of the molecular syntheses in which they are combined to form an organic association of even greater complexity. And molecules cannot of themselves account for the structure, no longer molecular but now cellular, in which they are combined and integrated. Lastly the cells, as such, cannot properly account for the unified, organic structure which a multicellular organism constitutes. The multiple does not adequately explain the synthesis in which it is integrated. If this multiple is called "matter," not in the physical sense but in its metaphysical meaning, we must then say that matter itself provides no explanation of the syntheses in which it is integrated, diversified, and brought to great heights of complexity at the level of living matter.

The synthesis transcends the elements which it integrates.

To say that matter "produces" or "creates" life and consciousness, is therefore even less that a paralogism. It is merely a *flatus vocis.*

From the simplest and most elementary level that we know, which is atomic, to the cellular and organic level, it appears that multiple matter, of itself, cannot account for the syntheses in which it is involved by a constant activity that impels it toward formations that are very complex. We must find some way to explain the simplest synthesis which we know in micro-physics, as well as the most complex synthesis based upon the most fully developed molecular structures.

If we consider the universe with regard to its existence and decide that it is not self-explanatory, we shall find that the same conclusion is inevitable when considered with reference to its evolution. As a matter of fact, with regard to the universe as it really is, existence and evolution are one and the same thing. We only distinguish them, in an academic way, for analytical purposes. But the empirical existence of the universe is a continuous evolution, a continuing synthesis incessantly evolving.

An explanation must first be provided for the existence of this multiple which is involved in a progressive synthesis, and then for this synthesis itself. The something *given* does not of itself account for its evolution and transformation.

But there is more to be said. This evolutionary development, as we pointed out, does not take place haphazardly, without a particular orientation. It proceeds in a very definite direction, moving toward structures that are increasingly complex. Father Teilhard de Chardin was doubtless the first to emphasize so forcefully this meaning of the law of cosmic development, this *orientation* of cosmic evolution, both biological and human, by his observation of the cosmic and biological phenomenon which is visible to all of us. The world is not evolving aimlessly or at random, but toward complex matter, and life, and consciousness.

When we say "toward" we are not necessarily guilty of anthropomorphism. We are simply using human language to signify a constant cosmic phenomenon. No doubt we must rid this word *toward* of any connotation of animistic or finalistic mythology. But there still remains the fact of an evolutionary process moving in a particular direction in the course of time.

Let us also note, in regard to material syntheses, that they should not be imagined as being similar to the way things are made by an artisan. The "synthesis" does not choose the corpuscular elements in order to construct a higher molecular structure with them, as a printer selects the type in his case to compose the *Iliad*. We must try to curtail the use of analogies of this kind, and all anthropomorphism in our representation of creation. Nevertheless, a certain analogy is legitimate in comparing the organic structure of a composition like the *Iliad*, with reference to the multiple elements which constitute it, and the molecular synthesis which integrates multiple elements. In both cases it may be affirmed that the elements themselves cannot sufficiently explain the total and meaningful synthesis in which they are integrated. *Chance* is certainly not the explanation of this synthesis, because the synthesis transcends the laws of chance. It is the destruction of the synthesis, the faults and flaws in its composition, which can properly be attributed to chance. The statistics of error would have reference to the laws of chance, but not the organic genesis, or the composition itself. Decomposition, or the increasing entropy of the system, falls under the laws of chance, but its organization does not.

There is a difference between the printer's type, relative to the synthesis of the Homeric poem, and the physical elements combined and integrated in the physical, atomic, molecular or cellular syntheses, because in the case of the printing plant there is a hand, visible and tangible, of the same order as the composed elements, which does the composing. In the case of natural physical syntheses, there is no hand. In other words, this means that the elements used by the printer, the pieces of type, possess a natural indifference with regard to their being combined in one synthesis or another. But insofar as natural physical matter is concerned, it seems that the situation is quite different. There is a pre-adaptation to the synthesis, a kind of "tendency" towards integration in an organic structure, inwrought, a propensity to formation from within. In other words, the synthesis is not brought about extrinsically, as in our handicrafts or industries, but in an immanent way.

However, from the metaphysical point of view, the synthesis, although immanent, is still also transcendent in regard to the elements which it integrates, simply because the synthesis is something other and more than the sum of its constituent parts.

The orientation of material syntheses toward increasingly complex states, and towards living and conscious organisms, gives evidence that this process is not a result of chance. The process is above the laws of chance although it does not contradict them. The statistical laws remain valid for all phenomena which *are not* phenomena of organization. But organization, which is the constant and fundamental process of the universe, is not subject to the laws of chance.

We began with the most external aspect of things, and likewise with existence, which is the most inward. In man we reach that part of the universe that is aware of existence interiorly, by reflection. If reflective consideration of the atom in terms of its origin and structure can be an adequate basis for metaphysical deliberation which, as we believe, leads to acknowledgment of a creative Being—and this will be the ultimate purpose of this inquiry—then, of course, a consideration of man as a being who is physical and alive, conscious and creative, will provide additional elements for a metaphysical elaboration that will lead us to the end of our quest. According as the universe becomes more complex and differentiated, and as its evolution proceeds in time, metaphysical reflection finds more and more material for an elucidation of the meaning and purpose of existence. For the metaphysician there is more to be found in living matter than in pre-living matter, as a source of instruction for his deliberations. There is more for him in the conscious and thinking organism than in the organism that is merely vegetative, and more in man, who is a conscious, rational and personal being, than in the animal. There is more at the *end* of the universe than there was at the beginning. Metaphysical research doubtless finds it rewarding to reflect upon the beginning, or rather the beginnings, but the primal periods of empirical physical reality are less significant than the later eras, and contemporary beginnings, which are called births, are richer in metaphysical substance than those first origins of the merely physical universe.

A metaphysical study of man will take us farther in our analysis than reflection on the physical universe alone, or even the animal world. With regard to man, our reflection can be dual. It will include the human phenomenon, outwardly, with a consideration of man as a being among many empirical beings that are given in our experience. And also man will be considered inwardly, since we ourselves are this very being whom we wish to examine. The two approaches are both fruitful and necessary. But the second will take us farther. It will carry us beyond the order of nature.

Man, the creature that is ourselves, is characterized by certain attributes traditionally called interiority, reflection, mediatized and well-considered activity, reflective speech, conceptual thought, etc.

We said that the multiple is unable to account for the syntheses in which it is integrated. Of itself, the multiple cannot be the explanation of material structures. Physical material structures cannot, per se, account for the living organic syntheses in which molecular structures are integrated. And living structures do not, of themselves, explain the reflection of consciousness, personal existence, or our freedom of action and thought. The superior cannot be explained by the inferior, as Auguste Comte pointed out. Personal existence, being properly human, could not possibly be explained in terms of any of the structures which prepare and sustain it. It is a paralogism, equivalent to a renunciation of the use of reason, to try to explain structured, organized matter by the multiple, or living matter by merely physical matter, or consciousness and reflection by the biological order. This would be an attempt to say that the lesser creates the greater, having within itself the means of producing the greater. Strictly speaking, this would be irrational and contrary to reason.

Actually, however, philosophical systems that uphold this proposition (which seems contrary to all rational exigence) seek refuge in an hypothesis that enables them to eliminate irrationality in its more obvious aspect from the proposition.

They say that matter produces life and consciousness by virtue of its natural endowments, because matter has the power to do this. Not only does it possess the power of self-generation, but it is endowed with the traditional attributes of the Absolute: aseity, eternity, infinity and ontological self-sufficiency. However, it also possesses the creative power of the Absolute. Within itself it has whatever is necessary for the creation of life and consciousness. In other words, matter *is* the Absolute: uncreated, eternal, self-sufficient and creative.

As a matter of fact, this materialism is pantheistic. It is a divinization of matter.

Once again we are faced with the choice between a philosophy based upon objective and positive reflection, an empirical analysis of material reality, and a philosophy which *adds* to this objective and scientific analysis, affirming the absolute and divinized character of matter, which is a wholly mythical assertion. As certain theorists of Marxism have remarked, we can choose between these two metaphysical systems, and we *must* choose one or the other. However, strictly speaking, nothing requires or obliges us, from a scrupulously rational point of view, to affirm the ontological self-sufficiency, the eternity and aseity of matter and motion. Rationally speaking, we have no compelling reason to say that matter is the Absolute. This is simply a metaphysical choice which itself rests upon no metaphysical principle or proof, but rather upon motivation of a different order, wholly human and political.

With these facts in mind, we can only conclude that from a strictly philosophical and rational point of view, which is the position we have taken, there is in fact nothing that could lead us to assert that matter is the Absolute, and is uncreated, or that it possesses within itself the necessary powers to produce life, consciousness, action and thought.

This secularized pantheism which we have just been considering is not the only form of pantheism which the philosopher will come upon in his search for a rational solution in regard to the world.

A more primitive and perhaps more widespread pantheism readily admits that there is a force operating in matter, transforming it and fashioning it into living matter, and finally bringing about its manifestations as life and thought. This pantheism concedes that the multiple cannot adequately explain the existence of material structures which are informed, organic and living. It recognizes that a *formal* principle is necessary to understand the nature of material substance. But this kind of pantheism sees no need to go beyond the idea which conceives of the formal, organizing principle, or the intelligence that is manifestly operative in the world, as being anything other than immanent.

This is the point of view of the pantheism of antiquity. The organizing, formal principle is purely immanent in matter and the universe. This was Aristotle's belief, for instance, and it was affirmed by the ancient Stoics as well. They believed that the universe is a god, a divine animal. Even Plato, as we noted, called the cosmos a sensible god.

A more subtle form of this pantheism, in the guise of evolution, consists in declaring that the intelligence which is immanent in the world, the Absolute that is operative within it, *is creating itself* in the process of creating the world. It is becoming what it is achieving and producing. Cosmogony is theogony. The evolution of nature is the evolution of God. The divine becomes self-conscious and produces itself by producing the world of reality. It is increasing and growing. The natural force which operates in mineral matter, in plants, and in animality, *becomes* consciousness. The Absolute would thus be incomplete at the beginning, and has been fashioning itself progressively. It would *not yet* be self-conscious at the level of pure matter, nor would it yet be life. This stage would only be reached when humanity appears.

This makes it necessary, once more, to choose between two forms of thought. One of them is based upon objective reality, and earnestly attempts to understand its implications, while the other presumptuously poses metaphysical affirmations that are unverifiable and mythical.

We can be certain that the immanent intelligence operating in nature, the organizing form which brings matter up to the level of organized and thinking matter, is *at least* equal to the maximum result achieved, that is to say, it is at least personal, conscious, and reflective, as man is, because, after all, it engendered man. This does not mean that it is *merely* conscious, personal and rational in the way that man is. But it does mean that we must concede to the Absolute both personality and thought, which are the appanage of man. The pantheism which we have just been citing makes this concession. Today, the

Absolute or divine is not merely an obscure, natural force, which the Germans called *Naturkraft*. The Absolute is now conscious and reflective.

The question, however, is to know whether this was always so, or if perhaps it has gradually become what it is today after being merely an organic force. In other words, we must determine whether the intelligence which is operative within the universe and in nature, in cosmic and biological evolution, before becoming manifest in man who reflects nature, is wholly immanent in the world and nature, or if it transcends them.

This is tantamount to asking whether or not the Absolute was complete and fully evolved before the creation and origin of the world and life and man. Or if perhaps the relationship between the world, nature and the Absolute is a relationship which in no way alters the identity between the Absolute and nature, or whether the Absolute is fundamentally *other* than nature which, in this case, would mean that the relationship between the Absolute and nature is one of creation.

Is it permissible for us to say that the Absolute was ever *less* in the past than it is today? Or that the Absolute cannot be in possession of its plenitude as long as the universe remains unfinished? Is man the revealer of the Absolute, and is the Absolute formed only by the genesis of the world and nature and man?

If we conceive of the Absolute as originally being less than it has become today, we encounter once again the idea that primal matter possessed within itself the power to produce life and consciousness. This was previously expressed in terms of materialism, but we now find it expressed at the level of pantheism and idealism. Actually, of course, from the rational point of view, it is the same idea, representing the same basic paralogism. It implies that the lesser contains the greater.

A mythical kind of thinking which does not hesitate to reject reason's demands could be given preference, but then, obviously, we would no longer be thinking rationally or philosophically. A definite choice must, in fact, be made. And the choice is between myth or reason.

The intelligence which has been operative in the world—and is still at work—organizing its multiple structure and constituting its intelligibility could not be purely immanent in whatever it organizes and constructs. The synthesis, we said, transcends the elements which it integrates. In a certain sense, it is independent of each particular element, as can be seen in living organisms. The physico-chemical elements of a living organism are completely renewed after a certain lapse of time.

Similarly, in a sense we may say that intelligence, personality and freedom transcend beings who are intelligent, personal and free. Organizing intelligence transcends all beings, considered individually; it is anterior and posterior to each, and continues its work when the individual, considered separately, passes away. It is not imprisoned in any of them. It accomplishes its work, and no creature determines this. Its limits are not assigned by any creature either. At the secondary or tertiary levels, it became manifest in one or another type of living organism. Later, it created other species, other forms of life. No living being can ever designate its limits without ridiculous presumption. This is no more possible now than it was in the distant past. Matter seems to be worked and penetrated, as Bergson remarked, by an impulsion of organizing consciousness, a creative intelligence.

Organizing intelligence is different from organized matter. Of itself, at its physical level, matter cannot fully account for the realizations in which it is included, transformed, and lifted to higher levels.

More can be said about this intelligence that is creatively operative in the world, and yet transcends it.

Creation is a gift. It is a gift to man. Existence is something given, and creation is a gift to all existing beings. We need not delve into the well-known themes of apologetics which the apostle Paul developed in his missions, teaching that the whole of creation is a gift, and nature is a kind of rejoicing.

This does not diminsh or ignore the problem of evil and suffering. But the gift of being and creation is primary. The problem of evil should not be underestimated, but it is a

secondary problem in relation to existence and life. There must
first be life before there can be any problem of evil, suffering and
death. The apologetical theme, whether employed skilfully or
not, thus possesses an undeniable, metaphysical foundation. We
can go so far as to say that the world, from a natural, rational
perspective, appears to be the manifestation of a creative love.
The Absolute is love, and is a gift to ourselves.

Let us be specific about this. Creation is a gift. First of all,
it is the gift of the being that we are, the gift of existence for
us who are alive. And then it is the gift of all the good things
of creation, provided for all created beings. It is the provision
of everything desired by these desiring creatures. The gift of
fruit for those who hunger; the gift of woman to man, and of man
to woman. The very beauty of creation also, for after all, creation
might have been dull, gray and miserly. But we find it mag-
nificent and superabundant, and beauty is its most universal
character. This beauty and profusion of creation indicates what
God is like. He is not the miserly and mournful deity, rancorous,
petty and mean, that so many treatises on spirituality would
like to force upon us. God is joy. His handiwork shows forth
His glory, and is vibrant with jubilation. We need not actually
characterize His work as Dionysian, which could be misleading,
but we can properly say that the Dionysian aspect of creation,
noted by the ancients, is certainly the work of the Creator. The
gift of woman, provided for man, is not the gift of a sullen,
puritanical or jealous God. Woman's beauty, and man's also,
which are a gift to both, can teach us a great deal about God.
Woman's countenance teaches us more about God than all the
treatises on spirituality. The delight and pleasure which man and
woman know in knowing one another are also the work of God,
even as they are His signs.

This beauty, joy and pleasure, partly constituting creation's
essence, must not blind us to whatever is horrible in the world.
We must never let ourselves become unconcerned about the evil
which is rampant everywhere. In our experience we find that
there is both good and evil, pleasure and pain. According to
their temperaments, authors minimize or emphasize one or the

other. Neither the beauty of the world nor the evil within it should be exaggerated, but it is well to keep ever in mind that they *both* will be found, everywhere and always.

Beginning at the biological level, something horrible seems to be ubiquitous, even if we do not resort to anthropormorphism by asserting that a beast experiences a kind of horror in seeing its offspring devoured before its eyes. In the animal world, devouring each other, and slaughter, is the law.

At the human level, things become worse. The lion which devours a gazelle is merely performing a biological, physiological act, inscribed in his very nature and wholly necessary.

But when man oppresses, kills or tortures man, he is not performing a necessary biological or physiological act. The human act is not purely biological. There is an addition of gratuitousness which is proper to the human and ethical level.

When we approach the problem of evil, we must make several distinctions:

There is a natural, biological level. Apparently there is evil, or at least pain, in the created world at the purely biological level. This evil is experienced, but it is not evil in the ethical sense. Man, in any case, is not responsible for this.

With the appearance of man, the biological level is not wholly abandoned, but continues in a certain sense and to some degree. Animality is prolonged in man, and there is still something biological in certain phenomena of human expansion, and perhaps even in war itself. The swarming of the hordes that invaded Asia Minor in the fourth millennium before our era is probably no different, essentially, than the vital and biological process whereby the lion devours the gazelle when he is hungry. There is a certain biological expansion which is natural, necessary and healthy.

However, man adds something new to all this. He brings the ethical dimension within him, and he brings evil, in the ethical sense, unnecessarily and perversely. He mutilates creation, and deforms his fellow-men; he disfigures himself. He destroys, slaughters, tortures, oppresses and degrades.

We should finally remember that whatever evil and pain may

be found in the created world, whether because of its structure itself or by the fault of man, this dread fact of evil does not annul the beauty, the excellence, the goodness and the delights of existence and creation, but is somehow additional to them in a complementary manner, so to speak. The fact of evil in no way detracts from the primordial fact of the excellence and splendor of creation. We must keep these two facts firmly in mind, simultaneously, if we wish to conceive of this phenomenon as it really is. If we see nothing but horror, like the gnostics, and say that the created world is fundamentally bad, we are simply raving. This would be a forgetting of all the peace and beauty of life. What we should emphasize in this respect, with reference to the problem of our knowledge of God, is that the primordial fact cannot be annulled (i.e., *the existence and excellence of the created world*) by any mention of the reality of evil everywhere present, for this evil is *within* the world of creation, inherently. The problem of evil cannot annul the rational proceedings whereby, beginning with the fact of the created world, we attain to a knowledge of God. The metaphysical problem of created being still remains, and the problem of evil cannot compel the mind to deny the uncreated and creative Being simply because of the evil that is partially prevalent in the created world.

This is not the place to examine the problem of evil, which must be the subject of another book. Let us merely point out, here and now, that there is an important difference between the evil that is inevitable, or physical evil, which apparently prevails throughout creation because of its structure, and the evil which is done by man, that is not necessary. Surely it is unfair to blame the Creator for man's evil deeds, if we really take man seriously as a being whom God has created to be the master of his destiny, and to play freely the role of a "created god," serving his apprenticeship for a divine vocation. The insufficiencies and incompleteness of creation, together with its pain and evil, remain a problem for us, but this problem should not properly be confused with the question of man's freedom and its bitter fruits.

In the course of this study the reader has doubtless felt many objections constantly rising within him. We have placed him in a triple quandary. Either the world has an absolute ground and cause, and consequently it is conceivable in the light of reason, (although this hypothesis is divisible, with one version affirming that the Absolute is purely immanent in the world, considered as a divinized world, *natura sive deus*; while the other version conceives of the Absolute as both immanent and transcendent, because creative). Or else the world has no absolute ground and cause, and we must be satisfied with ascertaining the existence of the reality that is there, without a "sufficient reason" and quite meaningless. We have confronted the reader with three types of metaphysics. One of them, in the tradition of the Upanishads and Spinoza, recognizes the Absolute as the foundation of reality but denies the transcendence and creative freedom of the Absolute. Another type, Judeo-Christian, also acknowledges the Absolute as the ground and cause of objective reality but conceives of the Absolute as a benevolent and personal Being, loving and free. The third metaphysical position denies the Absolute entirely, maintaining that we must be content with our knowledge of the contingent.

Because reality as a whole appears obviously incapable of accounting for its existence, structure, development and beauty, and because nothing in the world can sufficiently account for its own existence, birth and structure, does it follow that there is something or someone that is responsible for this existence, structure, evolution, expansion and beauty?

In our opinion, metaphysics of the pantheistic type can easily be refuted today if the witness and teaching of objective experience are accepted and taken seriously, at least to some degree. The pantheistic affirmation actually is based on nothing ascertainable or verifiable. It is a gnosis, transmitted through initiation. We have no facts, derived from real experience, to verify or establish it.

The philosophy which shuns the very idea of an absolute foundation of sensible reality is more difficult to vanquish. The whole essence of human reason is in question. Can human reason go all the way in its demand for intelligibility? Or must it abandon the quest for an absolute foundation, which Leibnitz called the "sufficient reason"? Must it limit itself, once again, to ascertainment of the fact of perceptible reality, its structure, evolution and splendor, and make no attempt to seek the intelligible ground and cause of that reality? Is this quest for ultimate intelligibility the ultimate illusion?

It did not seem that Kant's critique was decisive enough to halt us in our quest for absolute intelligibility. It is true, however, that only a transcendental critique could legitimately prohibit or prevent us from posing the question of "the radical origin of things." But we do not see how anyone can legitimately set limits to knowledge by considering the matter from within the conscious subject. For what possible reason can this quest, and this demand for integral intelligibility, be wholly condemned and refused? Is this done in the name of a psychological analysis? Then why isn't some analysis of reason offered which proves that the quest for the Absolute is entirely imaginary, a self-deception of the subject with regard to the end and purpose, clearly showing the concept of the Absolute to be false or meaningless or contradictory? Or is this done in the name of a political and economic analysis? But if this is the purpose, there should be a demonstration of this analysis which reduces the efforts of reason to a barren reflection on economic and political controversies. Ultimately it is still reason which passes judgment on these psychological and economic analyses, and it is reason, in the last resort, which will judge itself. Is the concept of the Absolute merely a pseudo-concept which implies a contradiction? This assertion requires proof. Any criticism will be welcome which can skim off the dross, or free the ore from the vein in which our thinking is imprisoned. All adverse criticism is clarifying.

Until these analyses are made in a convincing way, we certainly cannot see why we should renounce the spontaneous, natural exigence of our reason which is indeed seeking an absolute, rational ground and cause, and cannot rest content until it finds this ultimate and rational foundation.

To sum up, it is actually human reason which is in question. Does reason have the right to pursue its efforts in response to the promptings of its natural demand for an ultimate and absolute intelligibility? Or on the contrary, must reason inhibit this spontaneous tendency and refuse to undertake this quest which is so essential to it?

Denying the ultimate intelligibility which human reason seeks in "the radical origin of things" is really tantamount to reason's self-destruction. The world is inconceivable without a creating Absolute that is its ground and cause. But one can always refuse to conceive of the world itself!

Bergson developed the famous analyses which culminated in the dissolution of certain problems and concepts that are recognized as pseudo-problems and pseudo-concepts. Among these analyses, the one concerning the concept of nothingness is particularly important for our purpose. Bergson's criticism of this concept is tantamount to proving that *at least one being is necessary.* This is St. Anselm's proof in reverse, so to speak. *We cannot reject the concept of an absolute Being without denying our own reason.* We can, of course, repudiate our reason and also the demands it makes, as we can repudiate our life itself. But we would then be leaving the field that is proper to ourselves, which is precisely the field in which rational thought may be exercised. We can shun metaphysical problems, because we have little interest in such problems, or lack competence, or for the sake of method. But we cannot deny that these problems exist without also denying something that is important to reason. Only an analysis similar to the one in which Bergson showed that the idea of nothingness and chaos implies contradiction could compel reason to renounce the concept of an absolute Being. This demonstration, if it were possible, would indeed prove that reality is meaningless and that reason is merely a useless plaything, poorly constructed. However, such a demonstration is impossible, for reason cannot demonstrate its own incapacity or its fundamental defect without also destroying this demonstration itself.

Can we conceive of objective reality, the reality of experience, as the world whose existence is given as an indubitable fact, apart from the Absolute that is its ground and cause? Could it be possible that there is nothing more than "the world"? This is the question we have posed all through these pages.

At the purely physical level material reality, to be conceivable at all, requires a Being that is the source of its existence. Without this, we would have existence which "originates" and "emerges" in experience—being which is not itself the Absolute, and has no cause at all. To affirm that matter appears without a sufficient cause, and without any ontological foundation, is not only a repudiation of the use of reason, but is an assertion that is destructive of reason. Kant's critique objects that the causality which is valid within the field of our experience is not valid when we attempt to explain this experience itself. Transposed and set forth in another form, the same objection would maintain that the notion of causality, borrowed from our practical experience in the making of things, is not applicable at the metaphysical level. Let us therefore exclude this idea of causality. But it will still be true that if we posit the appearance of any reality whatsoever "in the midst of nothingness" or "following nothingness" without a Being that is its ground and cause, it is equivalent to reason's destruction, no matter how we approach or consider the matter.

This material reality, moreover, is not merely a fact. It is a universe of infinite complexity. Even more than the fact, and its factual existence, we must account for its structure. But here again, to affirm the existence of an intelligible structure or organism that is capable of living, while refusing to explain its ground and cause, is to abandon the use of reason. Or if we divinize matter in order to provide an ontological justification, thus declaring it to be eternal, we would be making a mythical assertion which has no basis in experience.

Matter is developing and evolving. A cosmic evolution is now known to us, which elevates matter toward degrees and forms of complexity that are increasingly greater. Unless we are willing to renounce the use of reason, and refuse to satisfy the most irrepressible exigence of rationality, we must explain this development and evolution also. It is a paralogism to say that matter, of itself, can sufficiently account for its evolution and development toward more and more complex states. This would mean that the multiple is adequately self-explanatory with regard to the complex syntheses in which it is included and integrated. It is an attempt to explain the greater by the lesser. Another effort may be made to elude the difficulty by divinizing the process—or evolution itself—but this is simply a flight into myth and irrational thinking. We have no reason to say that the cosmic process and evolution are the Absolute.

Life, similarly, requires an explanation. Something new, something greater, has appeared which cannot be explained in terms of the old or the pre-existent, which themselves would require explanation. Finally, man and human thought are something *given*, which neither life nor matter could account for ontologically. Something irreducible has appeared, and it would again be a repudiation and betrayal of reason's demands to pretend, as Marx and Engels attempted, to account for matter by referring only to matter itself. Of course, matter must then be endowed with all the attributes which are supposed to emerge from it.

The exigence of rationality confronts us with the hypothesis of an Absolute which is the only satisfactory explanation of reality as it appears to us. If it is objected that this exigence is factitious, deceptive and illusory, the renunciation of the use of reason is the only alternative. But serious reflection has not shown that the mind's deepest and most necessary requirement is simply pointless. We cannot have recourse to human reason in order to repudiate reason's demands. Like life itself, rationality is something given, which we can only use with discretion, reflectively and critically, but which we cannot call in question without repudiating all thought itself. The latter, likewise, is something given and irreducible. Reality is unthinkable without the Absolute, unless we are prepared to repudiate our thinking too. Perhaps this is the strength and essence of St. Anselm's argument, expressed in rather antiquated terms. If the existence of God is denied, our thinking necessarily contradicts itself.

God is that which cannot be doubted, the uniquely indubitable. It is God alone whose proper name is: I AM.

The denial of God implies a contradiction. It conceals a confusion of thought. *The fool hath said in his heart* . . . Biblical tradition teaches us that this denial, at the deep level of the heart's secrets, involves a choice and a decision.

We may make no attempt to consider the world in its totality, or in its beginning and evolution, as was mentioned in the first pages of this inquiry. We may refuse to pose the metaphysical problem in connection with our consideration of the cosmos. It is still obvious that the smallest datum of our most ordinary experience, no matter how minimal it may be—as for instance a little child who is conceived and is born, or a growing plant—will be quite enough to pose the problem in all its fullness: a being that did not pre-exist is now existent. Something new has appeared, a new being. To attain to knowledge of God metaphysical reflection will find that a consideration of the universal and daily phenomenon of a child's birth will be sufficient for its purpose. In the birth of a living being there is the same metaphysical mystery as in the origin of the world. A being that did not exist before is now brought into existence.

If there is any philosopher who is unwilling to think about this universal phenomenon of birth occurring everywhere around him, or any philosopher in his ivory tower who disregards nature entirely, let him consider his own birth and meditate upon the simple fact that his own existence had a beginning. This will sufficiently pose the problem of the Absolute to the fullest extent. We did not create ourselves.

We can even do without the concept of causality which is regarded doubtfully by many since Kant's critique. The principle of identity will be sufficient for our purpose. We have concentrated our whole analysis on the fact, now universally apparent, that we are living in a world which is subject to a system of genesis or evolving creation. In the course of time something *more* is continually appearing, which the former and lesser cannot adequately account for. Matter, of itself, cannot account for life.

And life, attaining to a certain stage in its evolution, cannot account for those thinking and personal monads that are human beings. At no time in its evolution can life itself be considered as a sufficient explanation of the subsequent stage which is the ingenious creation of new forms, more intricate and more complex, that are fashioned within it. *Natura naturata* cannot account for this creative process which continues to elevate and transform it. Created beings cannot serve as an explanation of the creative process which brings other beings into existence. And matter itself, considered in its primeval, pre-living forms, is not self-explanatory. In the hypothesis of a world that is limited in time, having an absolute beginning, nothingness could not possibly account for the emergence of material reality. Only being can account for being. In the hypothesis of eternal matter, we find that matter does not possess the attributes of a self-creative reality. It does not possess the attributes of the Absolute.

The principle of identity sufficiently manifests the absurdity of trying to explain being in terms of non-being, the greater by the lesser, or the new by the old. Therefore, we need make no reference to the disparaged image of the creative deity, and will only appeal to the most inalienable and irreducible exigence of rationality: the concept and import of being.

PART TWO

Knowledge of God Derived from Israel

. . . excluding the phenomenon of Christianity

If we now concentrate on a striking phenomenon that is localized
in space and time, directing our full attention to an historical
phenomenon as particular as the fact of Israel, we shall doubtless
offend the philosopher at the very start. However, from the
rational and philosophical point of view there is nothing illegitimate in this new approach to our problem. Israel is a phenomenon among phenomena, a fact among many facts, and
nothing that exists should remain foreign to philosophical reflection. Quite properly, philosophical reflection is interested in the
analysis of particular scientific phenomena, including the field of
physics and micro-physics as well as biology and psychology. It
applies itself to a consideration of the history of man and to
natural history also. In human history Israel constitutes a branch,
among others, which may contain certain lessons that are pertinent to the perspective which concerns us now. No ostracism
would be allowable or justifiable.

Let us therefore consider the phenomenon of Israel as something phenomenal. Primarily it is a history, relevant to history
in general. It is also an idea.

Both the history and the idea of Israel are distinctive because
each must be conceived as wholly characterized and differentiated by the discovery and knowledge of the Absolute as a
personal, creative Being whose relations with Israel are of a
personal kind.

71

Up to this point, our analysis has led us to the discovery of an Absolute that is indeed a subject and a personal being, since He is the source and origin of reflective, conscious and personal life. But our search for Him was our own quest and tentative seeking.

With Israel, and in Israel, a new phenomenon appears. If we may believe the scriptures of Israel, the Absolute Himself speaks to man, and comes seeking him. A dialogue is begun between the Absolute and man.

We must carefully consider what the prophets and sages of Israel tell us about the Absolute and His dialogue with man, and determine whether the philosopher of our day can, or even must, learn something from their teaching. We must therefore find the criterion of our adherence to their teaching, and see why a contemporary mind that is willing to make use of reason integrally and rigorously, can and must bear in mind what was said about the Absolute by nomadic Hebrews of some forty centuries ago, and by itinerant prophets of the eighth, seventh and sixth centuries before our era. In what way can the phenomenon of Israel concern philosophy or be of interest to it?

We must take the sayings and writings of these "prophets," and "inspired authors" and these men of wisdom into consideration, just as we give our consideration to the teachings of the Vedas, the Upanishads, the Presocratic philosophers, and Plato, Descartes or Kant.

We said that the history of Israel is distinctive because it was formed and wrought by a visitation, a dialogue, a relationship, between the Absolute and the Hebrew people. This, at least, is what Hebrew historiographers tell us in the Yahweh and Elohim traditions, and in Deuteronomy and the priestly code. And we are given the same assurances by the "journalists" of the time, those *nabis* whom we call "prophets." They were the interpreters of contemporary events, and analysts of the historical situations in which Israel was involved. However, they were not merely analysts, for they also proclaimed what was to follow. Their analysis of the historical situation, covering the past and the present as well as the future, was invariably based upon an awareness of a relationship between Israel and the Absolute, whom they called *Elohim*, (God) or *Yahweh*—a proper name which was revealed to Moses, according to one tradition, or a proper name already known, according to another. It is certain, in any case, that Moses recognized and acknowledged the identity between Yahweh and the God of his forefathers, the God of Abraham, Isaac and Jacob.

Continuously, from the beginnings of Israel to the Babylonian Captivity and the return from exile, the historical analyses of the interpreters of Israel's history were based upon this relationship between the living God and the people that He had created for Himself.

Israel knew that it had been specially created by the living God for a universal mission. "In *thee*," it was said to Abraham, "shall all the nations of the earth be blessed." In the history of creation, the origin of Israel is like a new stage in the creative process. Long after the creation of the world and of everything within it, and after the creation of man, we see the creation of Israel by the call addressed to Abraham. This was unquestionably a new creation, which was neither physical nor biological, nor was it simply human.

Israel was aware that it had been specially created to perform a task within the creative purpose of the living God, and knew that it was living a history that could never be dissociated from this task and mission.

To Abraham, the emigrant, there was promised a new land and a posterity—not in a natural sense, according to ordinary biological expectations, but in spite of the natural impossibility and transcending that impossibility. Abraham was an old man far advanced in years, and Sarah was barren, and also very old. But to Abraham it was promised that he would be the father of a people as numerous as the stars in the sky.

Certain nomadic tribes settled in the land of Canaan about the eighteenth and seventeenth centuries before our era. Others wandered into Egypt where they suffered captivity, oppression and humiliation. They were a foreign minority, considered as "unclean" by the people among whom they were living, a dis-

honored and exploited minority similar to the North African
sub-proletariat in France at the present time, or like certain
poverty-stricken Negro groups in America. A minority, restricted
to harsh labor, governed by the bludgeon, abused and oppressed.

A liberator arose, who persuaded this alien proletariat to
leave the land of slavery, and then led them into the wilderness.
Historiographers assure us that this deliverance by a liberator
was accomplished under the guidance of the God of Abraham,
the God of their forefathers. Moses, the man, achieved what was
humanly impossible, leading this enslaved people out of the
country in which they were exploited, rescuing them from the
hands of those who were using and abusing them for selfish
advantage. Hebrew historians all realized that there was truly
a supernatural intervention in this deliverance. With His mighty
arm the God of Israel had done what was impossible for men,
bringing about their escape from the land of Pharaoh and from
the land of their captivity.

No doubt the historiographers have embellished this epic
tale of the exodus from Egypt, but when we examine the most
ancient texts recounting it and consider the possibilities and the
impossibilities, keeping in mind the conditions of servitude and
the iron hand which imposed it, we understand and agree with
the historians of Israel that men alone could not have accomplished this escape from the house of their enslavement. There
is a sign in this, a sign of power, interpreted by the Hebrew
historians as a manifestation of God himself.

Following their sojourn in the wilderness, related differently
by the various sources which we possess, the Hebrew tribes,
having fled from Egypt, settled in the land of Canaan, which
had already been partially occupied by their ancestors. Here
again we must distinguish between the heroic folk-tale that is
related to us and the actual history which can be reconstructed
to some extent. The occupation of Canaan did not take place as
rapidly as the book of Joshua describes it. There was embellish-
ment in this narrative too. However, within the epic tale of the
conquest there is a real and certain historical nucleus. There was

a slow but victorious invasion of the land of Palestine by the tribes of Israel.

The forming of the nation of Israel was not accomplished until an *instruction* had been given them, making of them a "peculiar people" on the face of the earth. Israel received an instruction (*torah*) which transformed it inwardly in a fundamental manner. If we compare Israel with the neighboring pagan nations, we cannot fail to be impressed by the revolution that took place, considered from the human point of view or from the juridical, ethical and religious points of view. Quite appropriately, the book of Deuteronomy has Moses jubilantly declaring: "For what other nation is there so renowned that hath ceremonies, and just judgments, and all the law . . ." (4:8).

In Israel, humanity truly experienced a decisive moral conversion, and also a transformation of the mind. The repudiation of idolatry, the refusal to adore the things of this world as if they were the Absolute—the refusal to attribute divinity to the sun, the moon or the stars, the forces of nature, rivers or springs, trees, animals, pieces of wood, blocks of stone or metal—clearly attest that in regard to this advance humanity had at least attained to rationality. The Absolute is not to be found in anything empirical. Neither matter nor anything in the universe is the Absolute. By this single step of the Israelites humanity attained to a demystification which not all of our present-day philosophies have even yet achieved.

Rationality in thinking, and in interhuman relations, the discovery of justice as the principle of moral judgment, the repudiation of the mythology that demanded the sacrifice of the children of men, a respect for man and the created universe, all constitute the appanage accorded to Israel by that *torah* which Moses began to teach them, and which the later legislators were continually explaining, adapting and developing in terms of their contemporary circumstances.

Here also there is a phenomenon which is deserving of the philosopher's attention, for in this instance humanity attained to rationality and justice. Once more we confront a phenomenon which transcends the general and ordinary ascent of humanity, a phenomenon which apparently cannot be explained with reference to man alone.

As soon as they were established and settled in the land of Canaan, the nomadic tribes who had escaped from slavery in a foreign land began to "grow fat," eating and drinking their fill and forgetting the paradox of their great adventure. They forgot the impossible, which became the possible for them through the power of the living God. They forgot their God and broke the covenant contracted with Him, wallowing in the idolatry which flourished among their Palestinian neighbors. Their children were sacrificed to *Baal* and to *Moloch*. They prostituted themselves in the temples consecrated to astral divinities, and beneath every green tree or on every hill they worshipped the gods of the Canaanites and the Philistines.

The first part of Israel's history apparently ended in failure and defeat, for this people who had been created from nothing had forgotten the *sign* which consisted of their own existence, their past, and their presence in the Promised Land. They no longer remembered their God, the invisible Absolute who had created heaven and earth.

The second part of the history of Israel begins; and this is the history of sin and judgment. The prophets were raised up to tell Israel of its crime, and Israel's enemies harrassed the people of God time and again. The prophets interpreted this punishment as God's refusal to allow his people to annihilate themselves in the emptiness of paganism, destroying their national essence and purpose. War and persecution, prophecy and deliverance, were thereafter Israel's destiny. In this history that continues from the settlement in Canaan to the long Babylonian Captivity, and then to Roman oppression and the destruction of Jerusalem, the prophets rise up in every period to interpret this drama of the history of Israel in relation to the Living God, the Covenant, justice and truth. *The History of Israel is an encounter with God* who declares His will through the prophet, the man of the Spirit, and proclaims His judgment through the same prophet, foretelling the event that will come to pass. The history of Israel is like a prolonged empirical knowledge of God, an experience tirelessly repeated and carefully analyzed by the prophets in their teaching before occurring as an event in this history. It was an experience analyzed again after it happened, and then begun anew. The prophets called Israel a stiff-necked people, because they did not understand the experience, constantly repeated, in their flesh and blood. And the last of the prophets of Israel, Jesus the Galilean, who was to foretell the destruction of the second Temple, and of Jerusalem, would cry out despairingly, asking how long this people would lack understanding!

It is to this understanding and interpretation of the event that the prophets call us.

Interpretation of the event is regarded as an *experimentation*, similar to what occurs in the experimental sciences. A choice is proposed in advance between faithfulness and unfaithfulness to the covenant of Yahweh. The two ways are clearly marked out, leading to life or to death. Unfaithfulness entails the conditional abandonment of the people of God to their own strength. The prophet who is raised up in times of trouble analyzes not only the sin committed and the ensuing results, but also the help of God who, once again, will deliver Israel, His beloved people.

God arranges that the deliverance should occur in such circumstances that, humanly speaking, it would be impossible. Israel must not think that its own arm or its own might had rescued it, or ever suppose that its deliverance was accomplished by its human strength alone. To give only one example:

"And the Lord said to Gedeon: The people that are with thee are many, and Madian shall not be delivered into their hands: lest Israel should glory against me, and say: I was delivered by my own strength" (Judges 7:2). And Gedeon retained only three hundred men. The typical deliverance which God brings about is made especially apparent in the fight between David and Goliath. David proclaims the principle at stake before the event takes place, and in the presence of all the people: "And David said to the Philistine: Thou comest to me with a sword, and with

a spear, and with a shield: but I come to thee in the name of the
Lord of hosts, the God of the armies of Israel . . ." (I Kings
17:45).

This method of God, conquering through weakness, in order
that God may be known in His strength, is constant through all of
sacred history. This was truly *the method of the demonstration
of God to the Hebrew nation.* It was the barren woman whom
God made fecund, the humble and the weak whom He exalted,
while the mighty were put down from their seat. This was the
method praised in the Magnificat. From Moses and his tribe of
slaves escaping from the empire of Egypt to Jesus of Nazareth
and Paul, and the little handful of Galileans who confronted the
empire of Rome, proclaiming its downfall as the prophets had
heralded the ruin of Babylon, this was the invariable method of
God. His strength is made perfect in weakness, and Israel could
say with Paul, "For when I am weak, then am I powerful" (II
Cor. 12:10). Both Judaism and Christianity are paradoxical, and
this paradox of the victory of the weak in the world, like the little
band of Hebrew nomads or Galilean peasants overcoming the
world's mightiest nations, is the experimental demonstration of
God.

Let us cite still another example, among many, of this
method of the God of Israel. There was the victory of Achab,
king of Israel, over Benadad, king of Syria, related in III Kings
20:13: "And behold a prophet coming to Achab king of Israel,
said to him: Thus saith the Lord: Hast thou seen all this ex-
ceeding great multitude, behold I will deliver them into thy
hand this day: that thou mayest know that I am the Lord." The
promise and the principle are even more emphatic in verses 27
and 28: "And the children of Israel were mustered, and taking
victuals went out on the other side, and camped over against
them, like two little flocks of goats; but the Syrians filled the land.
And a man of God coming, said to the king of Israel: Thus saith
the Lord: Because the Syrians have said: The Lord is god of the
hills, but is not God of the valleys: I will deliver all this great
multitude into thy hand, and *you shall know that I am the Lord.*"

We see in both instances the constant presence of the

prophet, the man of God, who prepares the way for the experience, so to speak, revealing what may be expected, and interpreting its signficance.

The decisive difference between the holy scriptures of Israel and the sacred writings of the world's religions, is that Israel's Bible is a collection of documents and records which relate an *historical experience* that occurred in broad daylight and plain view, clearly visible to everyone. It is not a book that claims to reveal transcendent secrets in the name of an unverifiable gnosis. It is, instead, a record of concrete, historical experience. And this historical experience is continuing now. . . . The writings of Israel's historiographers and prophets are in our hands to help us understand and interpret the meaning of contemporary history which we are actually living and making at the present time.

At the beginning of this second part of our inquiry we asked what might be the criterion that would permit us to give serious attention to the teaching of the prophets of Israel concerning the Absolute. This criterion is precisely the one which made the prophets themselves consider as true the teaching which they received from God and then communicated to others. God did not ask the prophets to believe, or require the men of Israel to accept the prophets' teaching without discernment or uncritically, in simple credulity. God asked the prophets to believe Him because He performed an experimental demonstration of everything He told them, not the kind of demonstration which occurs in a private laboratory, but in broad daylight, plainly visible to everyone, and within history. The Bible refers to these demonstrations as *signs*. God gives the signs, and desires that they should be read, interpreted and understood. He does not require the people to believe any prophet who happens to come along. On the contrary, He provides a rule of discernment to distinguish the false from the true prophet, for it is the one whose sayings are fulfilled in history who is the true prophet.

In order that these signs be regarded as both usual and strong—and to make them imperative—God repeats them, but in doing this with the purpose of removing all doubt about them, He "hardens Pharaoh's heart" so that it becomes necessary to perform the demonstration of His power in a more striking way.

Israel is humanity in an empirical relationship with God. Consequently, the fact of Israel demands careful and close examination by the philosopher who is seeking knowledge of the Absolute.

The criteria which led us to a consideration of the teaching of the prophets and historiographers of Israel concerning God are the very criteria which convinced the prophets themselves. With these same prophets and historiographers of Israel we live over again, step by step, the whole experience of God with His chosen people, and of this people with their God.

The scripture which has been kept as a sequel to the book of the prophet Isaias and as a part of it, which is called the Second Isaias, lays stress on this methodological manifestation of God to mankind, in Israel, and particularly on knowledge of the fact preceding the event, a knowledge of the event which is communicated to the prophet, the man of God.

> Bring your cause near, saith the Lord: bring hither, if you have any thing to allege, saith the King of Jacob,
> Let them come and tell us all things that are to come: tell us the former things what they were: and we will set our heart upon them, and shall know the latter end of them, and tell us the things that are to come.
> Shew the things that are to come hereafter, and we shall know that ye are gods. Do ye also good or evil if you can: and let us speak, and see together.
> Behold, you are of nothing, and your work of that which hath no being: he that hath chosen you is an abomination.
> (Isaias 41: 21–24)

> All the nations are assembled together, and the tribes are gathered: who among you can declare this, and shall make us hear the former things? let them bring forth their witnesses, let them be justified, and hear, and say: It is truth.
> You are my witnesses, saith the Lord, and my servant whom I have chosen: that you may know, and believe me, and understand that I myself am. Before me there was no God formed, and after me there shall be none. I am, I am the Lord: and there is no saviour besides me. I have declared

and have saved. I have made it heard, and there was no strange one among you. You are my witnesses, saith the Lord, and I am God.

(Isaias 43: 9–12)

Thus saith the Lord the king of Israel, and his redeemer the Lord of hosts: I am the first, and I am the last, and besides me there is no God.

Who is like to me? let him call and declare: and let him set before me the order, since I appointed the ancient people: and the things to come, and that shall be hereafter, let them shew unto them.

Fear ye not, neither be ye troubled from that time I have made thee to hear, and have declared: you are my witnesses. Is there a God besides me, a maker, whom I have not known?

(Isaias 44: 6–8)

I have not spoken in secret, in a dark place of the earth: I have not said to the seed of Jacob: Seek me in vain. I am the Lord that speak justice, that declare right things.

Assemble yourselves, and come, and draw near together, ye that are saved of the Gentiles: they have no knowledge that set up the wood of their graven work, and pray to a god that cannot save.

Tell ye, and come, and consult together: who hath declared this from the beginning, who hath foretold this from that time? Have not I the Lord, and there is no God else besides me? A just God and a saviour, there is none besides me.

(Isaias 45: 19–21)

The former things of old I have declared, and they went forth out of my mouth, and I have made them to be heard: I did them suddenly and they came to pass.

For I knew that thou art stubborn, and thy neck is as an iron sinew, and thy forehead as brass.

I foretold thee of old, before they came to pass I told thee, lest thou shouldst say: My idols have done these things, and my graven and molten things have commanded them.

See now all the things which thou hast heard: but have you declared them? I have shewn thee new things from that time, and things are kept which thou knowest not:

They are created now, and not of old: and before the day,

when thou heardest them not, lest thou shouldst say: Behold I knew them.

(Isaias 48:3–7)

The prophet has the status of a mediator between the God of Israel and His people; he is the communicator of knowledge. Through his personal intervention we possess knowledge of God's purpose and we are present at the genesis of history. As the prophet Amos said, "For the Lord God doth nothing without revealing his secret to his servants the prophets" (Amos 3:7).

It was in Israel that the Absolute made Himself personally known to mankind. As Jesus was to say to the woman of Samaria, "salvation is of the Jews" (Jn. 4:22).

What do these prophets, these inspired teachers and wise men of Israel, tell us about God? What do they teach us about the Absolute?

First of all, they teach us that the Absolute is *other* than the world, as our own natural and rational reflection had led us to recognize—wholly other and different from the sensible, visible world with all that it contains. Nothing that pertains to the world, nor any element of it, is a god, or divine, or the uncreated, self-sufficient Absolute. Nor is the world as a whole any more divine than any of its elements. This is a repudiation of idolatry and consequently of fetishism; it is a denunciation of astrolatry, totemism, emperor-worship, etc. This cathartic critique is the necessary, negative preparation for the coming of positive knowledge. If the Absolute is wholly distinct from the world, the relation to the world and nature is not a modality of identity. Nature and the world are neither the Absolute nor a modality of the Absolute. The world is not the sensible god that Plato told of, nor the divine animal praised by the ancient Stoics. Nor is the world uncreated, as Aristotle suggested. It does not represent an alienation of divine substance, or an emanation either.

God is the wholly *other*, as Karl Barth has emphasized. He is not alienated or exiled in the world and nature. He is God, and does not become God in the genesis of the world. The relationship between God and the world is one of creation.

This relationship of creation is expressed in Hebrew by the

verb *bara*, which strangely enough, is used throughout the Bible only with reference to the creative action of God. The production done by man, which is fabrication, is expressed by another term, as for instance the word used to signify a potter's modeling.

God was recognized as the creator of the world and all that it contains beginning with the earliest prophets, like Amos, for example. God is the creator of heaven and earth, and of Israel, His chosen people. In the document which is called the priestly code (5th century), the metaphysics of creation is expressed in the most systematic way in the passage that we find at the very beginning of the Bible.

This creation is conceived and expressed as a free and sovereign act. There is no mention of any mythology of battles between gods, which haunted the Oriental religions of antiquity. Nor do we find the mythical tales of the origin, birth and destiny of the gods. Sometimes, in certain Psalms, there remains a literary vestige of these ancient folk-tales. But the unanimous doctrine of the prophets and the inspired theologians repudiates the mythology of ancient paganism.

Creation is therefore conceived as a *gift*, a manifestation, and as an expression of beauty and excellence. We no longer find the pessimism which obsessed certain ancient religions based upon dualism. The world is not the scene of an encounter between the principle of goodness and the principle of evil, locked in battle. The material world is not the place of exile for souls fallen into matter and bodies, as Orphism was to teach, and as the dualist religions of the Orient had declared.

Creation is jubilation, a manifestation of marvellous abundance, profusion, and beauty freely given. It is contemplation.

It is speech, particularly a gift of speech to him who is at creation's term: to man, called to know and name this creation, utilizing it and making it increase and multiply. Man is eminently a manifestation of the Absolute since he alone among all creatures is made "in the image and likeness" of the Absolute.

As soon as there was recognition of the Absolute as the Creator it became apparent that God is a gift, a discovery that was implicit in the original recognition. A Christian author expressed this later, "God is *agape*." God is love. Like so many other texts which have been juggled too often and perhaps repeated excessively, whether sincerely or not, this one has been tarnished and apparently debased. However, if we examine the whole idea that was developing and becoming consciously realized during the entire course of Israel's history, which must certainly be called sacred history, we shall see quite clearly that this text in the epistle of John is an expression of the essential aspect of the discovery of God which was achieved by these Hebrew nomads in the land of Canaan. There can be no metaphysics of creation without a theology of love. The purpose of creation is neither a lack, nor a need, nor an evolution of the deity. The purpose of creation is the *agape* of God. We hesitate to translate this Greek term which St. Paul and St. John both used in naming the love of God, because this word also has become tarnished and compromised in the sinfulness and deception of the world.

The New Testament has been compared to the Old as a revelation of love in contrast to the revelation of Law and severity. But we need only consider what is signified and implicit in creation alone, as the Old Testament conceives it, to see that this Marcionite contrasting gives us the wholly opposite meaning, and is error itself. The entire Old Testament conceives of the Lord, the God of the spirits of all flesh, the creator of heaven and earth, as a *loving* God. As a matter of fact, the Old Testament clearly gave expression to this love of God—paternal, maternal and romantic—the same love that is expressed by all the forms of human love in the Biblical images of the man who carries his sick lamb in his arms, or the father welcoming his beloved son, and the lover and his beloved in the Canticle of Canticles. Jesus made use of an image of the biblical type when He cried out, "Jerusalem, Jerusalem . . . how often would I have gathered together thy children, as the hen doth gather her chickens . . ." (Mt. 23:37). This is the love of God which is the source and fount of all the love in heaven and on earth.

This love is not an affectation. It is creative, infinite and demanding. God has not created man to become a painted puppet (as Plato remarked in *The Laws*) or a pampered animal. God did not create man for self-satisfaction or pleasant enslavement. God created man in His own image and likeness, to be a man resembling God Himself.

What does this mean and imply? What does it entail and require?

At this point we reach the part of theology of the living God which is the most difficult, most central and most essential, but the least taught and most misunderstood. It is expressed in both Judaism and Christianity.

Quite commonly creation is understood in the sense of human fabrication, as the production or making of some article, or an object or puppet. But this is crude confusion. However, there is still further confusion, equally crude and widespread, in conceiving of creation according to the analogy of despotism or servility. In this conception, God creates a being in order that the latter may do homage to Him. This analogy is suggested by countless political situations in the course of the centuries. But God is not a petty king with subjects surrounding His throne, to flatter Him and burn incense before Him. In the Old Testament, God's relation to man, contrary to Hegel's comment about it, is not the relationship of a master and his slave. It should instead be regarded, and is expressly signified, as a deliverance from slavery and a ransom.

Before all else, we must rid ourselves of these patriarchal and political analogies if we wish to understand the Christian and Jewish mystery in its full dimension.

It is not, therefore, a matter of creating a puppet, or an obedient slave, but a being who is made in God's image and likeness, that is to say, a god-like creature.

What does this involve?

God is a creator. Man must become a creator also. God is eternal, and man must become eternal too. God is God. Man must become divine.

But how can this be possible, since man is a created being? Man must appropriate creation and existence, the whole gift of God, to himself, in such a way that they become his very own.

In other words, he will have to consent to his own creation. He cannot be created in a purely passive way, for in that case he would not be made in the image and likeness of God. He was created to be a divine being, and must therefore act accordingly, as one who creates and gives. His appropriation of the gift of creation, bestowed upon him, should make a god-like being of man also. He must welcome the creative love of God, making it his own, in order that he may become a co-worker with God in creation. This gift must be appropriated to himself, and man must be willing to become divine by participation in the gift of God, which is His love.

Man must be transformed into divinity, becoming a new creature, conformable to the Spirit of God. But the gift of God is not to be sought or claimed as if it were an object to be seized. Man can only receive it as a gift making of him a being in the image and likeness of God. In any case, the creation of man can only be accomplished in two stages. First there is an immediate creation which we might call animal. And then a creation in which man cooperates in his own formation by willing acceptance of the life of God within him, and by consenting to a transformation that will change him from a living soul into a spiritual being. It is the animal and psychical which come first, according to St. Paul in his comments on Genesis. The spiritual comes last, and man must give his consent to this. It is necessary that man be born again, becoming a new creature, in order to participate in the life of God who is Spirit and freedom. It is essentially a question of appropriating to ourselves the creative freedom which is given to us, together with the Spirit whom we are bidden to share.

Many of our contemporaries, including some who are extremely clear-thinking and men of high spiritual ideals, now express a deep aversion to Christianity and Judaism because they do not see the real meaning of creation and imagine it to be like the creation that is commonly taught, resembling the human analogy of a servile relationship between the master and his slave, or even between a master and his dog! Quite understandably, these minds are offended in their human dignity. And in the presence of such teaching they speak quite legitimately in terms of a "religous alienation." There really is an alienation if man's relationship with God is conceived in this way.

The teaching that is commonly given is responsible in the highest degree, for it has largely neglected the riches contained in holy Scripture and the Fathers of the Church, preferring the scholasticism of the manuals in which the human, at its worst, takes precedence over the divine and over the word of God.

As a matter of fact, there is real alienation and humiliation if we are nothing but things in God's hands, or petty creatures called to spend all of eternity gorging ourselves with endless pleasures.

However, this is not what holy Scripture tells us. Instead, we are told that we are made in the very image and likeness of Almighty God, the Creator of all things. We are called to a divine destiny, and not to be like a dog beneath his master's table or like a sheltered slave. We are bidden to rise from the condition of a creature to the high level of the Creator. But we must be willing to allow the necessary change to occur within us. God cannot make us divine without our consent. Our freedom is the only thing that God cannot compel, because by coercing it He would destroy the divine essence that He wishes to create. God does not compel us. He invites and incites, urges us and calls us. Freedom is the principle and promise of our divine destiny. The human drama is something very different from a morality play portraying the struggle between good and evil, obedience and disobedience. It is the drama of the genesis of a divine creature who is free to refuse this creation but cannot cease to exist, because he is a created being. Blondel stated it well at the beginning of *L'Action*: "I am condemned to eternity." This drama is not only moral, and here again it is a debasement of the biblical mystery when the tragedy of creation and evil is reduced to the childish dimension of obedience and disobedience. It is certainly not a question of being well-behaved children. We shall not be justified by obedience. But it is essential that we be willing to become divine, and to participate in the personal and eternal life of God.

Our contemporaries need not fear that the call made to man in the Old and the New Testament is unworthy of them, or too modest. They should rather fear their reluctance to heed this high calling, for the soul must not be servile if we aspire to the life of God. Actually the teaching generally given shows that man is *afraid* of this truth which has been revealed to him, and that he reduces it to the measure of his servile and submissive soul through fear of the call that God addresses to him. The fear of God, which we find expressed all through the Old Testament, is also found in this fear of our divine vocation, which the parable depicts as a fear of seeking to increase and multiply the talent entrusted to us. This is a fear of cooperating with God in order to facilitate the growth of God's gift within us, which is the attainment of the fullness of the stature of Him in whom and with whom we are called to share in the personal life of God.

The Fathers of the Church, commenting on holy Scripture with fresh vision, were not afraid of the word of God, and they placed this doctrine of divinization (*theiôsis*) at the very center of their economy of creation and redemption.

The creative exigence of God's love is far greater than the manuals and sermons would have us believe. This exigence is far greater than all our hopes, even daring to desire for us such things as we would not dare to desire for ourselves. God's creative exigence cannot permit man to descend lower than his divine vocation.

This is what the Bible means when it tells us that God is a jealous God, a devouring fire. God is jealous of this vocation of ours for our own sake, and He is not willing that we be satisfied with a merely larval destiny requiring but little effort. He will not tolerate our wallowing in the emptiness of idolatry, the worship of those images which our hands have fashioned or our thoughts have conceived. He will not allow us to return to nothingness. The wrath of God is actually the love of God, intolerant of vanity, injustice, the crime of man against man, and against Himself. How badly the Bible has been read if we believe that the God of the Old Testament is a God of wrath and strictness, quite devoid of love! And how badly the New

Testament has been read if we have not found on every page
something of the wrath of God and the warning of God! In both
testaments the same wrath and the same love are expressed, the
same wrath expressing the same love.

The knowledge of God which we can derive from Israel is
the very knowledge of Almighty God to which Israel attained.
The criteria that will enable us to accept the knowledge attained
in Israel as valid are those which led Israel itself to consider this
revelation of God as authentic. God did not merely manifest
Himself to certain individuals, as to Abraham, the Patriarchs,
Moses, the prophets, etc. He provided intelligible *signs* that it
was His voice speaking, and that He was speaking to them.

We have seen that the manifestation of God to the people of
God occurred in a nearly experimental manner, by means of a
series of manifestations followed by historical experiences. Often,
the men of God who were favored by a personal manifestation
of God asked for a sign, proving that it was really God who had
visited them, and not merely a dream. In this way, by a manifestation of God, the positive knowledge of God was made available to His chosen people.

However, in the tradition of the prophets and the inspired
men of Israel there was also a negative way, critical and de-
nunciatory, and necessary in the approach to the living God.
This was the denunciation of idolatry and fetishism. This denunciation seems to be coextensive with the whole history of
revelation in the Old Testament. It is the necessary counterpart
of the positive knowledge of God, as we have already noted.

The critique of idolatry was rational, and could even be
called rationalistic. The prophets tell us that the gods of the
Gentiles are nullities, and in the Second Isaias we find the fiercest
denunciation of pagan religions. The statues before which the
worshippers bow down and to which they offer sacrifices, even
human sacrifices, are only pieces of wood or metal, carved and
painted by some artisan. But there is no breath in them, or life,
and they are unable to speak or think. They are merely *things*.
The artisan makes a boat or a table with the wood of a tree, and
then he makes an idol with whatever is left, and prostrates

himself before it, crying out: "This is my God!" It is this absurdity that the book of Exodus portrays with irony (32:3–4):
"And the people did what he had commanded, bringing the ear-
rings to Aaron. And when he had received them, he fashioned
them by founders' work, and made of them a molten calf. And
they said: These are thy gods, O Israel, that have brought thee
out of the land of Egypt." The Second Isaias tirelessly tries to
de-mythologize or, more simply, to demystify the system of
idolatry. Let us cite a typical passage in which the anonymous
prophet forcefully compares God the Creator with the god that
is made by human hands, and contrasts the God who speaks to
men and foretells the future with the gods that are nothing but
perishable things:

> Thus saith the Lord the king of Israel, and his redeemer the
> Lord of hosts: I am the first, and I am the last, and besides
> me there is no God. Who is like to me? let him call and
> declare: and let him set before me the order, since I ap-
> pointed the ancient people: and the things to come, and that
> shall be hereafter, let them shew unto them.
> Fear ye not neither be ye troubled, from that time I have
> made thee to hear, and have declared: you are my witnesses.
> Is there a God besides me, a maker, whom I have not known?
> The makers of idols are all of them nothing, and their best
> beloved things shall not profit them. They are their wit-
> nesses, that they do not see, nor understand, that they may
> be ashamed.
> Who hath formed a god, and made a graven thing that is
> profitable for nothing?
> Behold, all the partakers thereof shall be confounded: for
> the makers are men: they shall all assemble together, they
> shall stand and fear, and shall be confounded together.
> The smith hath wrought with his file, with coals, and with
> hammers he hath formed it, and hath wrought with the
> strength of his arm: he shall hunger and faint, he shall
> drink no water and shall be weary.
> The carpenter hath stretched out his rule, he hath formed
> it with a plane: he hath made it with corners, and hath
> fashioned it round with the compass: and he hath made the

image of a man as it were a beautiful man dwelling in a
house.

He hath cut down cedars, taken the holm, and the oak that
stood among the trees of the forest: he hath planted the pine
tree, which the rain hath nourished.

And it hath served men for fuel: he took thereof, and
warmed himself: and he kindled it, and baked bread: but
of the rest he made a god, and adored it: he made a graven
thing and bowed down before it.

Part of it he burnt with fire, and with part of it he dressed
his meat: he boiled pottage and was filled, and was warmed,
and said: Aha, I am warm, I have seen the fire.

But the residue thereof he made a god, and a graven thing
for himself: he boweth down before it, and adoreth it, and
prayeth unto it, saying: Deliver me, for thou art my God.

They have not known, nor understood: for their eyes are
covered that they may not see, and that they may not understand with their heart.

They do not consider in their mind, nor know, nor have the
thought to say: I have burnt part of it in the fire, and I have
baked bread upon the coals thereof: I have broiled fish and
have eaten, and of the residue thereof shall I make an idol?
shall I fall down before the stock of a tree?

Part thereof is ashes: his foolish heart adoreth it, and he will
not save his soul, nor say: Perhaps there is a lie in my right
hand.

(Isaias 44: 6–20)

This passage, which sums up the general reasoning of the
prophets, presents us with an analysis that is a *reduction*: the
idol is reduced to its material substance and to a fabricated
object. The prophets analyze the process of making idols in
order to prove that there is no good reason to adore anything
which has been made with our own hands. They point back to
the idol's origin to demystify it completely.

Let us also note the beautiful and more ancient text of
Jeremias, contrasting the God who creates with the gods that
are made by men:

For the laws of the people are vain: for the works of the

hand of the workman hath cut a tree out of the forest with
an axe.

He hath decked it with silver and gold: he hath put it
together with nails and hammers, that it may not fall asunder.
They are framed after the likeness of a palm tree, and shall
not speak: they must be carried to be removed, because they
cannot go. Therefore fear them not, for they can neither do
evil nor good.

They shall be all proved together to be senseless and foolish:
the doctrine of their vanity is wood.

Silver spread into plates is brought from Tharsis, and gold
from Ophaz: the work of the artificer, and of the hand of the
coppersmith: violet and purple is their clothing: all these
things are the work of artificers.

But the Lord is the true God: he is the living God, and the
everlasting king: at his wrath the earth shall tremble, and
the nations shall not be able to abide his threatening.

He that maketh the earth by his power, that prepareth the
world by his wisdom, and stretcheth out the heavens by
his knowledge.

Every man is become a fool for knowledge, every artist is
confounded in his graven idol: for what he hath cast is false,
and there is no spirit in them.

They are vain things, and a ridiculous work: in the time of
their visitation they shall perish.

The portion of Jacob is not like these: for it is he who formed
all things: and Israel is the rod of his inheritance: the Lord
of hosts is his name.

(Jeremias 10: 3–5; 8–10; 12, 14–16).

This critique of fetishism, which is relatively easy (at least
from our later point of view), is not, however, without relevance
to ourselves. Because while we are not likely to make idols of
metal, stone or wood, the whole process of creating false gods is
still with us. However, it is now interior. It is no longer wood,
but rather with our thought alone, that is to say, with our desires
and affections, our consciousness and the unconscious also, and
with our imagination, that we make divinities for ourselves,
before which we bow down adoringly, whether as individuals
or collectively.

If the critique of fetishism seems quite easy to us, the denunciation of astrolatry, on the other hand, represented an act of rationalism that makes those ancient men deserving of high praise. No longer considering the sun, the moon, the stars and the forces of nature as divinities, but regarding them as merely created things, was an accomplishment whose rational and philosophical content must not be underestimated. Towards the sixth and fifth centuries before our era certain Greek philosophers dared, at the risk of their lives, to direct their criticism against the ancient animism that was universally prevalent. It was also against this cosmic and biological animism that the prophets and the whole tradition of Israel rose up in protest. In Greece, among some of the Presocratics, as in Palestine, there was a striving for rationality, which was occasionally resisted by the priests of the local cults. But in Israel it was victorious, while in ancient Greece the critique of the rationalists was to be submerged by the reflux of the cosmic mystics who regarded the universe as a god and considered the stars as divine substances.

We must therefore recognize the rational content of biblical theology and its cathartic influence. It actually eliminated all the ancient religions insofar as these religions were matters of concern to it, and with the means that were available it brought about the demystification and rationalization to which we have now attained, partly through this same theology, and partly through our experimental science. While the ancient Hebrews declared that the sun, the moon, the earth and the stars are not divinities, and based their certainty upon metaphysical and theological principles, we, for our part, possess this knowledge because we explore the universe with the means that are available to experimental science.

Within biblical theology there is a rational theology, at least of a negative kind: nothing in this visible, sensible world is the Absolute, and nothing is divine.

In the first part of this inquiry we saw that human thought has actually oscillated between two principal affirmations. Either the world is in some sense identified with the Absolute, or is the Absolute itself, or else it is wholly distinct from the Absolute, but was created by the Absolute. In both cases, it is acknowledged that the world is founded upon an Absolute. The difference consists essentially in the way the Absolute is conceived, and its relation to the world.

It seems that it is but rarely that the idea has been proposed and expressed, as it is in some contemporary philosophy, that the world has no absolute ground and cause whatever, because there is no Absolute. This thesis, if it were conceivable, that is to say, if it did not entail a ruinous contradiction of itself within its own internal logic, would constitute an authentic atheism, which we could justifiably call absolute atheism, without any play upon words.

The question, as we have seen, is to know whether this thesis is really a *concept,* and whether it does not imply an oscillation between two incompatible points of view, perhaps even representing, per se, a destruction of reason, a suppression of the exercise and exigence that constitute reasoning itself.

We found that Marxism did not seem to be a "pure" atheism, but was more like a hidden pantheism, as though ashamed of something, since the metaphysics of Marx and Engels recognizes that there is indeed an Absolute, which is the universe or matter, endowed with the attributes of divinity, aseity, eternity and creative power.

Pure atheism, in our opinion, is found in the philosophies of the absurd, which assert that the existing world is founded upon *nothing.*

Biblical thought, for its part, developed a critique of what it considered to be false representations of the Absolute and the divine, and erroneous relations between the Absolute and the sensible world. By eliminating these false representations of the divine, it encouraged a line of reasoning which consisted in a conception of the Absolute considered as transcendent, free and creative. Biblical thought does not propose a new representation of the Absolute, different from those of the past, but strictly forbids any and *all* representation. It calls us to an act of the intellect by which we free ourselves from representations in order to know the Absolute as the creator of the world and of all representations. A *hidden* God means that He cannot be imagined or be the object of any representation, because He is not sensible or visible in any respect. He is the one by whom the visible and empirical exists.

Doubtless, if we wish to do so, we can inhibit reason's quest which carries us from the experience of existence to the discernment of the intelligible foundation of all existence. We can probably deny this inner demand for intelligibility, rejecting the act of our own reason. But we could no longer say that we are performing a rational act. Reason is something given, an exigence that is given to us. We can avail ourselves of it, or refuse to use it at all. It is conceivable that some men suffer because of this human condition, in which, inevitably, experience and reason can only be something given. Conceivably, from the perspective of rationality, this "something given" requires a ground and cause, and some philosophers refuse to admit that this could be anything other than the human self. It is this condition of a created being who receives everything he uses, which they call "religious alienation." But we must determine whether this flight into the mythical affirmation of the substantial divinity of the self, or the refusal to undertake the quest for the ground and cause of whatever is given, really is the best solution to the difficulty which they encounter.

As we noted before, biblical theology sets forth a metaphysics of creation which is not humiliating to man and is in no sense an "alienation," but much to the contrary it offers a way of advance, a *"theiôsis."* The fact of being born and having a father does not seem to constitute a reason for depriving oneself of growth and of creative participation in the very life of the Father of the universe. We realize, of course, that the teaching which is most commonly given today is inclined to imbue the theology of the living God with representations of a paternalistic, sociological type, which are very apt to make those who possess no liking for the patriarchal regime feel a deep distaste for the whole theology of the universal fatherhood of God.

In this respect, representations and words must be transcended in order to grasp what they signify. The analogy of the fatherhood of God is not of much worth unless it is clarified. This fatherhood essentially signifies the free, creative love of God. And this creative love, let us point out again, does not aim to produce merely obedient children, or men who are children eternally, but to communicate existence and the gift of Love to beings who are able to receive the Absolute.

This ability to receive the Absolute means that they are also creators, in the image and likeness of God. To him who has, it will be given. From him who has not, there will be taken away even that which he has. The tree that does not bring forth good fruit will be cut down.

The knowledge of God in the Old Testament conception is not simply mental or speculative. In other words, knowledge, as it is conceived in the Old Testament and in the New, is not dissociated. It is man who knows, and not merely his "reason" understood as a separate function—which would constitute a "different dimension," so to speak. It is *man* who knows. Knowledge of God, in the Old Testament, possesses a *moral* content. And this knowledge is not possible without a concurrence of human freedom. Knowledge of God does not exist apart from *justice*, and justice *is* the knowledge of God. The whole doctrine of the knowledge of God is summed up in this passage from Jeremias: "He judged the cause of the poor and needy for his own good: was it not therefore because he knew me, saith the Lord?" (Jer. 22:16).

According to the formulation which the New Testament gives to this idea, the knowledge of God is charity. It does not exist apart from charity. It is a knowledge of the charity of God, a realization of the fact that God is charity, and it is therefore a participation in the charity of God. (We have used the word *charity* in its full biblical sense, of course, and not in its debased modern meaning.)

PART THREE

Knowledge of God Derived from the New Testament

Our point of departure in this inquiry was the consideration of reality in the broadest sense, material reality regarded from the perspective of its simple existence. We concentrated upon the evolution of matter which tends to organize increasingly complex structures, and then directed our attention to living matter, which is such a small part of the universe, and to humanity, a single branch of the immense tree of life. In Part Two, we chose to think about a very small nation, the smallest of all nations according to Deuteronomy, and we gave special consideration to certain men, including Abraham, Moses, David and the prophets.

But now again we shall narrow the scope of our reflection, and will concentrate our whole attention on Jesus of Nazareth.

Jesus was born in a common milieu, in the province of Judea, then occupied by the Roman invaders. Following his years of childhood and youth, of which we know very little, he began to teach. He preached to the multitudes, while other men—including fishermen, a tax-collector in the service of the occupying power, peasants and workers—followed him. He asked them to forsake everything if they wished to follow him. And straightway they left their boats and nets, the tax-gatherer's post, and even their families.

What was Jesus telling these people? The kingdom of

heaven is at hand, now is the time accomplished, repent and believe in the glad tidings.

What was the meaning of all this?

The kingdom of God, in biblical tradition, was to be the final fulfillment that was glimpsed by the prophets of human history. The knowledge of God would fill the earth as the sea covers the sands of the deep. Justice would reign, and God would wipe away all tears. The wolf would dwell with the lamb, and no cry or complaint would be heard again in the new Jerusalem. Nor would there be any more oppression. It would be the reign of justice.

The time is at hand? What did this mean?

It meant that the work of God in man cannot be accomplished all in a moment, and that time is a part of creation, not in an accessory or factitious way, but essential to it. The creation of the world took time, a very long time. The genesis of life took time. The appearance of humanity required a long preparation at the biological level. However, humanity, appearing at a particular moment in the history of life, at the high point of life's evolution, was not suddenly constituted in the fullness of its essence and vocation. From the biblical point of view, as from the Pauline, humanity was created gradually, according to a plan, and in stages, in which there was a beginning and a sequence. Humanity emerged from animality in what was doubtless a sudden divergence and mutation. But a long, slow development, psychical, mental and sociological, was necessary before mankind was finally ready to receive and bear the seed of the new humanity that was to become the people of God. Abraham, only twice nineteen centuries ago, left Ur of the Chaldees. That was only yesterday. Humanity had already had a long history before the word of God was addressed to Abraham, telling him: "Go forth out of thy country, and from thy kindred, and out of thy father's house, and come into the land which I shall shew thee" (Gen. 12:1). And Abraham departed, not knowing where he was going.

After Abraham's day, the nation that was promised to him gradually increased. They were instructed in the doctrine of the living God and went through the painful but joyous experience of learning what it meant to be chosen as a prophetic people by God Himself. Like the prophets who, on many occasions, tried to decline this call, saying that they were weak and sinful men, and wanted God to find someone else to teach His word, this people likewise often regretted that they were not a nation like all the others. A prophet tells them that the word which had risen in their heart would not be fulfilled and they would be a people "like all the peoples of the earth."

But Israel was not merely one nation among many. It was the rought draft, the seed, the venture of a radically new humanity, a second creation. It was the creation of a humanity capable of hearing the Word of God, and able to respond to Him, entering into a personal relationship with Him; a humanity, moreover, capable of receiving the Holy Spirit and of being profoundly transformed by that Spirit. It was a humanity consenting to this radical transformation, this second creation, by which man becomes a son of God, capable of receiving God, and made in His own image and likeness.

Time was needed for this people to increase in numbers, and to enable them, progressively, to be the bearers of more and more of this new learning which was the knowledge of God. It took time to bring about their repudiation of the ancient oriental religions, ridding themselves of the myths, rites, cruelty, superstitions, taboos and all that was primitive and infantile. This emergence from their primitive and superstitious past, and their achievement of rationality, did not occur suddenly. It was accomplished very slowly and with difficulty. Israel was learning about God through experience, and God was testing His chosen people empirically. Holy Scripture has preserved the memory of the deeds and words of the conjugal experience between the living God and this small portion of humanity, the Hebrew people.

"The time is accomplished" means that something has reached completion and maturity. A threshold has been crossed, and something wholly new can now appear, which was being prepared during the course of many centuries. What is this something, wholly new? "The kingdom of God is at hand."

What were the signs that were given by this man, Jesus, to

convince his disciples and the multitudes? He healed the sick, the blind, the deaf and the paralytics. He did things that man is not able to do.

He taught, but not like the doctors and rabbis, who relied upon the writings of others, and on the commentaries on commentaries of those writings. He taught as one having authority. And what did he say? To the paralytic he said, "Thy sins are forgiven thee," which only God can say. He taught that the poor and the persecuted, and those who hunger for justice, the meek, the peacemakers, are blessed, for they possess the promise of eternal life, and the kingdom of God is open to them. He spoke in the same authoritative and paradoxical way about the harlots who enter the kingdom before the priests and doctors of the Law. He was glad to keep company with those who were regarded as "disreputable people" by the harsh, puritanical code of those days. He taught truths, not concerning the present, physical universe, but rather the world that lay hidden in the hearts of men, the kingdom of God, that would soon become manifest. The kingdom of God was likened to a tiny seed that grows into an immense tree. To Abraham it had been promised that his posterity would become a great nation, and all the nations of the earth would be blessed in him. The kingdom is like the leaven which a woman put into a few measures of meal, till the whole was leavened. Israel leavens all of humanity, transforming and supernaturalizing it. The kingdom of God is like a pearl of great price which, when it is found, a man will sell all that he possesses in order to buy.

It is as difficult for a rich man to enter the kingdom of God as for a camel to pass through the eye of a needle. A man must be born again, not by a biological birth of flesh and blood, but of the Spirit. Whosoever would save his life shall lose it, but whosoever is willing to lose his life, shall find it, even more abundantly. If the seed does not die, it abides alone, but if it falls into the ground and dies, it brings forth much fruit. The kingdom of God is for those who are like little children, understanding what the wise and the learned do not understand. Whosoever has, to him it will be given, but whosoever has not, from him will be taken away even that which he has. Every tree that does not bring forth good fruit will be cut down and cast into the fire.

All these truths pertaining to the kingdom of God, which is already present among us and within us, together with these laws which could perhaps be called "theorems" of the kingdom, enable the man who understands them to explore their deep content which, for once, both legitimately and without exaggeration, may be considered inexhaustible. Even at the human level, these theorems of the kingdom of God are true and verifiable. Indeed, in human affairs, in the order of our successful endeavor, whosoever would save his life shall lose it, and whosoever is willing to risk the loss of it, shall find it superabundantly. And if anyone leaves his father and mother, his brothers and sisters, for the sake of the kingdom of God, he will find brothers and sisters, fathers and mothers, a hundredfold, even in this present life.

Jesus constantly appealed to men's understanding. He pleaded for it, and his frequent reproach was the question, "Do you not understand?" or "Have you no understanding?"

"Do you not yet believe?" was also his question to men. This faith for which he was pleading, had nothing in common with credulity. It was quite specifically the mind's approach to truth, the recognition of that truth, the assent of the convinced mind, and not in any sense a surrender of intelligence, or *sacrificium intellectus*. Opposition between faith and reason is fundamentally non-Christian and contrary to the Gospel. This famous polarity must be dismissed from our thinking if we are to understand what faith means in the New Testament, which uses this term in the sense of intelligence itself, in its act and its successful attainment, and as meaning the very knowledge of the truth that is taught, and a recognition of the identity and authority of the Teacher. According to the Gospels, belief is the discovery and understanding of the truth that is proposed to us. To the child who is learning how to swim we explain that because of natural laws there is no reason to be afraid, and if he will only make a few simple movements he will be able to swim. But the child is perhaps still afraid. He shrinks back, and does not seem to believe us. But finally the moment comes when he discovers that what he was told is really possible, after all. He believes, and now he is able to swim. In this case, it cannot be said that faith is opposed to reason, or is even distinguished from it. It is, in fact, almost identical, although faith is something other than understanding, being the mind's assent to the truth which it discerns and adherence to the truth which is perceived and acknowledged. This is the meaning of the term *pistis, pistuein,* in the Gospels. In the Fourth Gospel faith and knowledge are constantly associated as if inseparable: "They have known and they have believed that thou art the son of the living God."

It was indeed to our understanding that Jesus appealed, and not to our credulity. Contrary to what some people would have us believe, credulity and poor judgment are in no sense an acceptable homage to God. Truth certainly does not require that man be stupid, nor need he scuttle his reason which, on the contrary, is essential to the attainment of the knowledge of God. In Western civilization, for several centuries, we have been familiar with a tradition which claims to base the knowledge of God on a disparagement of reason, a repulsing of the demand for rationality and intelligibility. This mistaken contempt for reason has no more basis in biblical and evangelical tradition than the disparagement of our corporeal and biological life. The Master of the New Testament does not ask us to "humiliate" our reason, but to open our minds and to understand.

The laws of the kingdom of God which were taught by Jesus and the theorems which constitute the laws of the spiritual life must be considered in themselves and judged in the light of their intrinsic truth, or we might even say that they must be experienced. They are the laws of successful achievement and of life, a success which is mediated by an apparent, immediate failure. Whosoever would save his life, shall lose it. If the seed does not die, it abides alone.

All of biblical theology is paradoxical. It was tiny Israel that was destined to transform the whole of humanity. It was the weak, who lacked chariots and horses, who would triumph over the mighty and the powerful of this world. The wisdom of God has always been deliberately paradoxical in relation to the wisdom of men. The method of Jesus brought paradox to its apex, and the dialectics of immediate failure which constitutes the necessary stage preceding eternal victory, like the law of the seed which must die in order to bring forth much fruit, is that truth which no mind can conceive until it has gone beyond the order of immediate evidence. It was not the man, momentarily rich, who possessed within himself the hope of the greatest wealth, but rather the man who was poor. It was not the empire of Rome, armed to the teeth like Goliath, which could hope to endure perpetually, but a little band of Galilean peasants who incited troublesome incidents in Rome itself, where the police ordered their banishment before carrying out a repression that was far more severe. In all of this we see something constantly dialectical in the method of God which constitutes an ironical attitude in regard to the forces, the power, the wealth and wisdom of this present world.

This irony is intelligence itself. And in regard to the "values" of this present world, it is wisdom itself.

Hegelian jargon would call this irony a kind of negativity with regard to this world's values. It is a dissolvent, and that is why the world despises the wisdom of the Gospel, even as the sick man detests the psychoanalyst who make him aware of his own contradictions, and as the totalitarian state hates those whom it calls "intellectuals." On three different scales and levels we find an analogous process. Intelligence is despised. Truth is hated from the very depths of their souls by those who wish to preserve their private interests, their way of life and their possessions, their mental outlook and their habits, against the truth. There is opposition and warfare between man and truth which requires that we reconsider the simple correspondence, which we had accepted as a working hypothesis, between rational research and truth. Rationality and intelligence are discovered to be inseparable from acquiescence in rationality and truth. Just as the psychoanalyst cannot compel the sick man to exercise clear introspection and learn the truth about himself, for the same reason metaphysical truth cannot coerce the human mind, for the mind is always free to turn its gaze away from the truth. In other words, there is a procedure that is based upon *bad faith*. In regard to indifferent things like numbers or quantities, the mind remains "pure." Freedom does not intervene. But we are well aware how decisive our consent or refusal to face the truth can be, especially when the truths that are most vital to ourselves are concerned. Consider, for instance, from a purely epistemological point of view all that occurs in the world of politics!

As a matter of fact, human intelligence does not "function" with invariable simplicity. The act of the intellect is not dissociable from an assent to truth by our most secret freedom. The refusal to understand, or a lack of understanding, cannot be explained apart from those secret longings of the heart which are mentioned in the New Testament. Rationality is unattainable without a moral conversion, which the Bible calls a "renewing of the heart," that is to say, of both our freedom and our intelligence, which the New Testament translates as a "renewal of the mind."

Jesus gave men a teaching which revealed the laws that govern the economy of eternal life, the kingdom of God. He gave them signs by rendering sight to the blind and hearing to the deaf.

Gradually, he revealed who he was. This was expressed in the language and terminology of Jewish messianism and the apocalypse. We need not attempt to examine this gradual revelation of himself to his disciples, to the extent that this would now be possible, for such a study would properly pertain to the theology of the New Testament.

We shall, however, take note of a few salient points.

In several texts, Jesus expressly identified himself with Yahweh, the God of Israel and of his forefathers. "Jerusalem, Jerusalem, that killest the prophets, and stonest them that are sent to thee, how often would I have gathered thy children as the bird doth her brood under her wings, and thou wouldst not?" (Luke 13:34). In this passage, for instance, Jesus clearly identifies himself with the God of Israel's history. He reveals himself as being the God who called His chosen people to justice, faithfulness and truth, through the mediation of His servants, the prophets.

In the Old Testament, the God of Israel said of Himself, speaking through the prophets, "Hear, O Israel, the Lord our God is one Lord. . . . Therefore thou art magnified, O Lord God: because there is none like to thee, neither is there any God besides thee. . . . I know there is no God in all the earth, but only in Israel, . . . (there are many texts: Deut. 6:4, 7:9, 32:39; II Kings 7:22; III Kings 8:23, 8:60; IV Kings 5:15, 19:15; Psalm 46:11, 86:10; Isaias 43:10, 44:6, 44:8, 45:6, 45:22).

In the Fourth Gospel we find passages which sound very similar to those we have cited, and seem to allude to that Word of the creative God, speaking of himself to man, and saying, "I AM."

"For if you believe not that I am he," (*hóti egó eimí*, John 8:24); "then shall you know, that I am he" (John 8:28). "At present I tell you, before it comes to pass: that when it shall come to pass, you may believe that I am he" (*hóti egó eimí*, John 13:19).

This last text plainly recalls to mind the reasoning of the Second Isaias, who based his demonstration of the God of Israel on the fact that only the God of Israel predicted what was going to happen in the future.

There is a text in the Fourth Gospel which asserts the pre-existence of Jesus: "before Abraham was made, I am" (John 8:58, *egó eimí*).

In these passages, Jesus is revealed as being Yahweh, the God of Israel.

In other passages, Jesus made a distinction between his "Father" and himself, and refers to himself as one who was "sent," or as the "son," or as having a "mission" or task to perform. However, over and beyond this distinction, he repeatedly declares that he and the Father are one.

In an essay that is strictly a philosophical inquiry, we cannot enter upon a study of the New Testament. More specifically, we can only devote some of our thought to the theology of the New Testament from a philosophical and rational point of view, by a provisional and methodological consideration of this theological datum as a phenomenon which we can analyze and try to elucidate. This procedure, however, cannot forbid our giving our ultimate adherence to it. Philosophical reflection on the New Testament would require a profound study, not only of the texts of the New Testament itself, but also of the documents of the early Christian tradition which express a gradual awareness and grasp of the theological content of the New Testament.

How Jesus attempted to teach men about himself, revealing that he was actually the One who had said I AM, and as being Yahweh, the God of Israel (while on the other hand being distinct from his Father) is a theological problem that was deeply meditated by Christians during all of the first centuries of our era. They made a real effort to recount and express the revelation and manifestation of God in man, without any omission or diminution of the deposit of faith. Beginning with the New Testament, and until the Councils of Nicea and Chalcedon, Christian thought was devoted to an attempt to understand and express as correctly as possible how Jesus was in fact the living God who revealed Himself, even though he was also distinct from the Father. God was not completely immersed in this incarnation by which He became manifest. The life of God is not solitary. Our knowledge of God, derived from Jesus, includes the Church's reflection on this gradual awareness of both the unity and the distinction of the Son and the Father and the Holy Spirit. Nothing is more admirable than this tentative procedure by which Christian thought, in a series of gradual approximations, expressed the revealed mystery of God, manifesting Himself in person, although He was not alienated in this manifestation or incarnation (contrary to Hegel's opinion, who saw in the incarnation, and creation also, an alienation of the Absolute). The Christian philosopher cannot dispense himself from continuing this effort of the Church which seeks to give expression to her thought and to whatever God has revealed to her.

We cannot now enter upon such a philosophical reflection on the development of the dogma of the Trinity, but we wish to point out that any philosophical reflection on the knowledge of God, to be complete, cannot omit this, in as much as reflection of this kind should encompass all of reality, even if this requires consideration of the properly supernatural order of the gratuitous manifestation of God to man. The philosopher must give his consent to this consideration, if objective reality demands it of him. The fact of Christianity and the Church constitutes this objective reality. Let us simply note the difference, in this respect, between the Christian idea of the incarnation and the theme which is often found in the religions of both India and ancient Greece, telling of the manifestation of a god to man, and appearing in human form.

The manifestations of divinities, in the tradition of India, for instance, can be unlimited in number. According to certain Hindu theosophists, Jesus was *one* of the manifestations of the Absolute, in the same way as the others, whether before him or after him. But from the Christian point of view, this incarnation of the Absolute was *unique*. But this is not the most important difference.

According to the Christian religion the Absolute came into this world which is His creation to manifest Himself by being born among men and assuming human nature completely, so that He is wholly divine and wholly human, true God and true man. God did not merely assume the *appearance* of humanity, but real and concrete human nature. Christ is consubstantial with his Father, because of his divinity, and consubstantial with ourselves, because of his humanity, and is like us in all things, except sin. In this respect, the Christian idea of the incarnation, defined by the Council of Chalcedon, is fundamentally distinguished from all the theophanies of the non-Christian religions.

From a strictly philosophical point of view, is this manifestation of God, the invisible Creator, quite unacceptable and contradictory, as Spinoza thought? Is it impossible for the Absolute to be manifested to man, if this requires that the Absolute become incarnate in order to speak to man? Is the infinite incapable of self-manifestation in the particular? Can the One who is Spirit manifest Himself by being born in the sensible, bodily and material condition of humanity? Or is this impossible? A neoplatonist would ask whether matter is not too impure for the immersion of the One. And furthermore, why would the Absolute come to us? It is we who must return to the Absolute, by forsaking this world of matter and cares and exile.

A whole series of principles, which are perhaps prejudices, militate against a manifestation of the Absolute to man. A particular conception of matter, considered as radically foreign, or even opposed in its principle to the divine, constitutes the first obstacle. A certain conception of transcendence, perhaps influenced by a spatial perspective, cannot admit that the One who is *outside* and *above* the world would enter *into* the world. And certainly more decisive is the conception of the Absolute and the divine which was held by Plato, Aristotle, and Plotinus. They believed that the divine is the object of our longing and our nostalgia, to which we aspire to return. But it would never have occurred to Plato, Aristotle or Plotinus to imagine that the Absolute is concerned about us. The idea of a creation, like the idea that the Absolute is love, was first expressed in the biblical tradition.

If we dismiss these metaphysical objections which rest upon psychoanalysable presuppositions that are not irreducible, it is quite evident that with regard to this gift of the Absolute to man we cannot logically or rationally decide beforehand what is possible or impossible. As with creation, which would have seemed impossible if we had asked the opinion of a witness *before* it occurred, the incarnation does not fall within the scope of our knowledge of the possible or the impossible. We can only pass judgment concerning the possible in the presence of something existent, and as Bergson has shown, then only in retrospect. Life would doubtless have seemed impossible to a witness in any period preceding its appearance, and in Pre-Cambrian times man's emergence would surely have seemed impossible also. By the very fact that creation does bring forth something radically new, it must not be pre-judged as being either possible or impossible. We can do no more than ascertain the fact and decide that it must have been possible, since it actually occurs.

The incarnation, like creation, is a gift. The philosopher can analyze its timeliness and the pre-adaptations, indicating the natural desire that pervades all of creation for a supernatural end, the longing for the visitation of the Absolute, and a union and assimilation with the Absolute. But the philosopher, as such, cannot prejudge the gift of the Absolute, which is freedom. This freedom is what theologians call the gratuitousness of the supernatural gift. Quite justly, they cling tenaciously to this.

Inversely, if man cannot prejudge the gift of God, neither can he prejudge the limits or extent of God's gift, or determine the impossibilities which could not be overcome by the Absolute.

The incarnation, which was the manifestation of the Absolute to man under the only possible form, that is to say, in human nature, is not the only gift by which the Absolute is made known to us. While creation is the first of these gifts and the first manifestation, the indwelling of man by the Spirit of God is a gift that enables man to know God interiorly, and also lifts man above the purely natural level.

This communication of the Holy Spirit, given according to modalities which we are unable to determine before the origin of the people of God (if we are to believe the biblical pre-history which the theologian of the Yahweh tradition sets forth before beginning the history of the chosen people), becomes an integral part of an economy which determines the genesis of the people of God. The *nabi*, the prophet, is a "man of the Spirit," a man on whom the Holy Spirit and the word of God descend.

"O that all the people might prophesy, and that the Lord would give them his spirit!" (Numbers 11:29). This saying, attributed to Moses, defines the vocation of the people of God whom God looks upon as a "priestly kingdom, and a holy nation" (Exodus 19:6).

This interiority of the spirit of God in man is a gift which alone makes possible a knowledge of God that is not merely an inference or induction proceeding from something created. As St. Paul tells us, only the Spirit of God knows the things of God. Our knowledge of God is only possible because God knows us. Our understanding of the incarnation and the person of Jesus, and the reading of the signs which Jesus gives men, and which he constitutes, is only possible (the New Testament assures us) through this action of the indwelling Holy Spirit in us, enabling us to discern the meaning of all that is inscribed in the person, the sayings and deeds of Jesus. "Because flesh and blood hath not revealed it to thee, but my Father who is in heaven" (Matthew 16:17).

At this point we definitely pass beyond the order of philosophical reflection, properly so called, and our own efforts come to an end.

Let us note that this communication of the Holy Spirit to man, this secret and intimate relationship between the Absolute and man, by the Spirit of God in direct communication with the spirit of man, poses the problem of knowledge which we were considering at the beginning of this essay, but in new terms.

Kant posed the problem of metaphysical knowledge in terms of solitude, by supposing the existence of a conscious subject that is apparently in no relationship with a creative Absolute whatsoever. In Kant's opinion, is this conscious subject created or uncreated? The Critique of Pure Reason is treated apart from this alternative which, however, is inevitable and must at least be posed, if only to be excluded for the sake of method, and provisionally, but in a well-considered manner.

We have seen that our point of departure had to be something *given*, which is the empirical datum, on the one hand, and the rational and conscious subject on the other. We cannot pretend that this datum is not something given, or that we are its real creators. And we had to analyze what this datum implies, presupposes, and previously requires, in order to be conceivable. A reflective analysis seemed capable of leading us to acknowledgment that this datum implies a creative Absolute.

Consideration of a part, spatially tiny but qualitatively exceptional, of the given world, comprising Israel and the phenomenon of the Jewish prophets, led us to admit that the Absolute really enters into a diagnostic relationship with man, a relationship of love.

Consideration of the fact of Christianity and the person of Jesus led us to agree that the Absolute really can be made manifest in man.

But our understanding of what Jesus really is only becomes possible through a motion of the divine intelligence.

Could not the same thing be said about our own reasoning in its entirety, and might not all reflection be influenced secretly, under the motion of the creative Spirit? In other words, should the rational reflection which we wished to pursue in a strictly philosophical way still be considered purely *natural*, or is it previously structured or influenced by a supernatural assistance?

Man is not a self-created subject, nor is he an uncreated subject. If he is a created conscious subject, his creation is not merely an act which took place in the past, but is actually occurring now, continuously, for the creative process is still operative in us all. At the same time, the act of creation gives man a creative vocation and creative freedom, which enables us to appropriate this gift to ourselves, making it our own, so that we also may become creators in the very image and likeness of our Creator.

According to this hypothesis, our knowledge is no more solitary than our existence, our life or our motion. Our act of knowledge, which is certainly our own, is however conjoined with the creative act which endows us with consciousness.

Kant's critique poses the problem of knowledge within an hypothesis of isolation. It is not surprising that there is no way out of this solitary isolation, originally posed.

Our speculative reflection is still purely rational, philosophical, and valid in principle, if properly carried out, for any man who makes rigorous use of his reason. However, we cannot go so far as to say that our philosophical and rational thinking occurs in a radically solitary manner, as if we were cut off from the initial creative act which constitutes us as thinking subjects, or that it takes place in a purely "natural" way, as if we were entirely alone in our quest for truth. If man is a created being, favored with a divine vocation, he is not subject to the conditions of "pure nature" exclusively. And if man is indwelled and actuated by the Holy Spirit, he is no longer to be considered only in terms of his own human nature. Instead, he possesses a created nature which is in process of being supernaturalized, transformed, continuously created, gradually united with God.

Philosophical reflection is inevitably subject to the same conditions as humanity in general.

Jesus of Nazareth taught that it is not given to anyone to know *who* he is, unless this knowledge be given by his Father . . . "flesh and blood hath not revealed it to thee, but my Father who is in heaven" (Matthew 16:17). Without the Spirit of God in man, it is not possible to know who Jesus is, for it is the Spirit of God that gives understanding.

Knowledge is no more the act of man alone than his existence or his life, for man is not uncreated.

Philosophical reflection can proceed as far as ascertainment of the necessity of this gift of the Other in order that the created being may gradually come to know the uncreated Being.

Jesus revealed himself to man as the manifestation of the Absolute. Not only did he teach the laws of growth and of the economy of the kingdom of God, which is already present in our midst—although it has not yet been revealed what we shall be—and not only did he teach the laws of the Reality that was yet to come, which he alone could teach, but in his countenance men saw the express image of the Absolute that was revealed and manifested through the mediation of men of God, in the history of God's chosen people. But in Jesus the Absolute was manifested in person. In him we recognize the same divine Being; the One who speaks and reveals Himself to us through the history of the Yahweh and Elohim traditions, and through the books of the prophets of Israel, which are still in our possession. It is the same Being and the same Spirit, the same sovereign power, of whose presence within himself Jesus was both aware and certain. "Heaven and earth shall pass away, but my words shall not pass away. . . . I say to you, if you shall have faith, and stagger not . . . you shall say to this mountain: Take up and cast thyself into the sea, it shall be done (Matthew 21:21). . . . Before Abraham was made, I am . . . that whatsoever you shall ask of the Father in my name, he may give it you" (John 15:16).

This was simply a manifestation of his own awareness of invincible omnipotence.

This same method of God which characterizes His intervention, as recorded in the books of the Old Testament, indicates that His omnipotence is made manifest in gentleness and with discretion. God has been reproached because He would not adopt an imperious manner in His self-revelation. Instead of a lowly birth in a stable at Bethlehem, there are those who would have preferred a solemn and thundering descent in the very center of Rome, the great capital of the Empire. But the manner of God is never an imperious, Napoleonic pose. From the very beginning, the Old Testament shows us that God's method and "manner" may be described and characterized as a combination of omnipotence and weakness in the means employed, with gentleness and discretion also. God did not descend upon humanity with an army of archangels. He was *born* among men, as unnoticeably as any other birth. Beginning with the nomadic tribe of Abraham, father of the emigrants, God revealed the plan of His salvation for all mankind, the birth of the people of God who were to become the kingdom of God. Like the mustard seed, which is the tiniest of all seeds, Israel was the smallest nation of all, as Deuteronomy tells us. And yet, from Israel has come the knowledge of God, the birth of a new humanity, and the beginning of a new creation that will never end. Salvation is of the Jews. Constantly, in the history of the people of God, the dialectics of weakness triumphing over the strength of the world was to be utilized and verified, with David forever striking down Goliath.

The God of Israel does not need to throw dust in our eyes, like the false gods devised by man's imagination. His power is combined with gentleness, and He manifests Himself in meekness and silence as a still small voice, "a whistling of a gentle air" (III Kings 19:12).

There is a question of "propriety" in this. The Holy Spirit is not incompatible with propriety, and the latter is not incongruous with grace. The work of God is beauty, because it proceeds from Him who is subsistent beauty and the source of everything beautiful. All the beauty on earth and in heaven had its origin in Him. And in manifesting Himself, God could not appear in the gawdy attire of tinsel and vanity.

While the apocalyptic writings of the later Judaism diverged considerably from biblical aesthetics, and both the apocalyptic and apocryphal scriptures became stereotyped in style, so far removed from the style of the Yahweh tradition, as in Amos, Isaias and Jeremias, we find that Jesus continued the ancient tradition and again revealed the dialectics of power becoming manifest in weakness. Even as the coming of the Messias according to the expectation of the apocryphal apocalypses would have been the sign of a false advent, we see the unmistakable mark of the God of Abraham, and the seal of the God of David, in the birth at Bethlehem. God was born among men, without drums or trumpets. His revelation of Himself was gradual because He respected the creature He had made. Jesus generally forbade those whom he had healed to tell it to anyone, and he commanded his disciples to keep silence concerning anything he told them about himself.

If we considered things as a level which might be called phenomenological, we could say that the *character* of Jesus, as it becomes apparent through the four Gospels which were written by men, continues and completes the character of Yahweh, according as this was revealed through the books, records, documents and prophecies of the Old Testament. Always, it was *the same Spirit* who manifested Himself in both the Old and the New Testaments, the same doctrine, the same severity and austerity, together with the same gentleness, the same infinite gravity because of man's sin, the same indulgence toward weakness, the same strictness and the same sweetness. An awesome God, but also a God of love. Why did anyone ever try to portray Jesus as a demure and effeminate teacher? The truth is that Jesus was a stern master of men as we see him in the four Gospels and in the Apocalypse of John. How could anyone fail to recognize that the God of Abraham, the God and terror of Jacob, is also the loving God who took Israel, His beloved people, into His arms, to feed and comfort and care for them? These artificial contrasts between the God of Abraham and of Jesus arise from a misunderstanding of the books of both the Old Testament and the New, but this is a misunderstanding which can hardly be considered involuntary or in good faith.

In the Old Testament, as in the New, the Lord God, creator of heaven and earth, appears as a terrifying God—"it is a fearful thing to fall into the hands of the living God"—and also like a God who loves this creature man, whom He has made. His very essence was defined in the epistle of John: God is *agape*. But this *agape* is severe, because it is love, and love requires and demands justice. *Agape* is not complacency or weakness, nor is it a willingness to allow man to degrade himself, but a stern demand, an infinite demand, for the sake of man, who is not called to become a pampered puppet, but rather a divine being, with God Himself.

God is not therefore an emasculating God in the Old Testament, nor is He all sweetness in the New. In both, He is the same God who creates us to become divine beings and not mere slaves, and is more concerned about our own beatitude than we are. He will not let us sell our heritage for a mess of pottage. Love is not complacent, but demanding. It is not a toleration of baseness, but the requirement of holiness. The so-called antinomy between the God of justice and the God of love, the God of the Old Testament and the God of the New, is thus dispelled.

The knowledge of God which we derive from Jesus of Nazareth, whom Christians call the *Meschiha*, that is to say, the Anointed of God, is not limited to a knowledge of God revealed through his person, his deeds and words, as recorded in the four books of Matthew, Mark, Luke and John.

Knowledge of God, through Jesus and in Jesus, also comes to us through those who are engrafted in Jesus, their Lord, and live the life of the Spirit of the Lord so fully that they can now say, "It is now no longer that I live, but Christ lives in me" (Gal. 2:20).

Those who are called saints are men and women who indeed live by the very life of the incarnate God. They are transformed in Him, and made wholly new in a profound and radical way, by Him and within Him.

A consideration of the phenomenon of Christian sanctity is quite pertinent to philosophy and rational reflection. But it is a phenomenon which leads us beyond the phenomenal, and although rational reflection may be able to account for whatever is exceptional, novel and original in this phenomenon, and perhaps describe some of the aspects which define it, we cannot say that such reflection can adequately explain the inexhaustible and radically new elements within it. The phenomena of faith, hope and charity can, of course, be ascertained, at least exteriorly, and their metaphysical structure can also be analyzed. Their effects can be described. But the content itself cannot be fully known by a rational reflection that is external to the phenomena, simply because this content is radically new in relation to what was previously given. Faith, hope and charity can be known reflectively by the subject who has been personally renewed in them. But the subject who possesses this immediate knowledge also knows that faith, hope and charity do not appertain to the order of created things or nature. They are a participation in the uncreated order of the Creator, who freely creates all new things. He makes a new heart in man, and pours out His Spirit on all flesh. Purely rational philosophical reflection leads us to the threshold of the Christian phenomenon, analyzing whatever falls within its proper scope. But the element of newness in Christianity can only be known by a transformed mind and a new understanding.

Human reason, accustomed to thinking in terms of created things, finds itself confronting a wholly new creation in Israel and Christianity, as the prophets had said. It is indeed a new humanity which, through the mediation of the Spirit of God coming to dwell within us, now enters into a personal relationship with the Uncreated. The indwelling in His people by Almighty God is the true definition of Israel, the people of God and the Church.

The fact of Israel, the people of God, constituting the promise and seed of a new humanity, and the phenomenon of Christianity and the Church, cannot be appraised by a reasoning mind which has been exclusively concerned about the old creation. Opposition between "reason" and "faith" could therefore be reduced to the kind of opposition that originates in a mind accustomed to knowledge of certain data, but which refuses to recognize this newness of being and new creation, requiring a renewal of reason itself, *anakainôsis tou noûs*, according to St. Paul. A person who will not believe in the creation of the new, because of the hold of the familiar and the old, will also be unable to believe in the possibility of the original creation in general, or of the world, or even in the possibility of his own creation, as St. Justin remarked (I *Apol.* XIX).

This indicates an habitual fallacy of thought, which claims the right to predetermine what is possible or impossible. This is done in the name of a reality already given and long existent, as if reality had not always been subject to innovation and new creation, and consequently (going further and further back in time) the mind would ultimately be able to acknowledge only nothingness, if its opinion were asked! Being or existence would have seemed impossible at that point, and the world's creation, with all it comprises, would indeed seem like a contradiction.

CONCLUSION

The inquiry which we have tried to set forth in this essay has been, in our opinion, a rational endeavor. It has been a speculative procedure, logical, well-considered, and with no "qualifying leap into the absurd" as Kierkegaard would say.

Contrary to contemporary fideism, we are convinced that a knowledge of God is really possible by a correct use of human reason, beginning with the fact of creation.

We do not mean that we, ourselves, have succeeded in correctly analyzing the logical structure of these proceedings. But we do believe that the endeavor itself is at least possible, and that it is not necessary to ask the unbeliever to make a "leap" that is actually equivalent to a *sacrificium intellectus*. It certainly does not require a repudiation of the use of our intelligence, but on the contrary we need to develop that intelligence and keep an open mind which must be liberated from certain inveterate fallacies.

Nor are we suggesting that this quest, this *itinerarium mentis ad Deum*, could have reached its destination without the guidance of Judaism and Christianity, or if there had been no manifestation of the Absolute to man.

In our day, we can attempt a reflective analysis of the proceedings by which we attain to knowledge of the Absolute, and we can analyze the logical structure of this endeavor, but only because the Absolute has in fact already been revealed. In any case, prior to revelation, or outside its phylum, it does not seem that the human mind has ventured, or even knew how to make this discovery, unless perhaps in rare instances. This conclusion is inevitable to the extent that we are able to judge by the philosophical documents that are still available to us, revealing the thought of antiquity, whether Egyptian, Sumerian, Assyro-Babylonian, Hindu or Greek. This is the question which was asked by the author of the *Epistle to Diognetus*: "Was there ever anyone, among men, who knew what God is, before He came Himself? It was God Himself who was manifested" (*To Diognetus,* VIII, Marrou transl., p. 71).

Our journey toward the discovery of God, with the world as our starting-point, is apparently a rational process, but actually it does not seem that such journeys of the mind were ever made before or outside the phylum of Judaism and Christianity. This does not detract from the logical structure of the proceedings by which thought attains to knowledge of a creative Absolute. It only proves that the human mind is congenitally affected by a weakness or difficulty in conceiving of reality, life, the spiritual or the new. Bergson said that human intelligence is characterized by a natural incomprehension of life, evolution and creation. No doubt this assertion should be modified by showing, for instance, that mathematical thought has been able to effect a change enabling it to grasp the idea of motion, which Bergson did not consider possible. Human intelligence is not hopelessly incapable of understanding ideas of motion, life, freedom, or the sudden rise of unforeseeable newness. However, it does stumble over the fact of creation as it occurs, and life, motion and freedom are also mental stumbling-blocks. It is a transformation of our understanding that is required.

As a matter of fact, knowledge of the Absolute conceived as transcendent, free and creative, was only achieved among the people of God. Once again, however, this does not prove that human intelligence, of itself, is incapable of attaining to this knowledge. It only proves that a transformation of the mind is necessary for its attainment. After long hesitation, Bergson called this transformed intelligence "intuition." But the Bible simply calls it "understanding," (*bina*). To designate the Bergsonian "intelligence" that is characterized "by a natural incomprehension of life," the Bible uses such terms and expressions as stupidity, lack of understanding, etc.

It is most difficult to make any kind of rationalist admit that a transformation of the mind is necessary to the attainment of truth, which is the very object of intelligence, especially if he is more or less inclined to consider reason as an organon, ready made, a kind of thinking machine which we need only turn toward reality. But we know that modern physics and biology also have required a renewal of reason. Rationality is defined in terms of whatever exists, following upon the discovery of the existent, but no longer a priori. Reality will doubtless demand many more renewals in our conception of rationality.

With regard to the properly supernatural order, which far transcends the order of physical or biological knowledge, and is a matter of spiritual knowledge instead, the transformation or conversion required for attaining to understanding is even more demanding. It is moral.

There is therefore some distance or margin between what seems possible for human intelligence and its actual achievements, outside the historical phylum of the people of God and their influence. Today, human thought has rid itself of the phantoms and illusions whose exorcism does not seem to exceed our natural powers, but it is through the influence of Jewish and Christian biblical thought that it has succeeded in overcoming whatever was still primitive and pre-logical within it, as for instance, the worship of the stars, or of men. . . .

This margin between the natural power of the mind and its actual deficiencies can only be explained by an analysis which takes into account the mind's human, psychological, ethical, political and other conditioning. As the Bible very definitely disclosed, the mind is not separable from the whole man, nor from his conduct and behavior in general. An analysis of deficient intelligence, or a phenomenology of stupidity, is not possible without an ethical or moral analysis, discerning the secret motives which govern man's behavior and thought.

When we began this essay, we indicated that we would have to take for granted both objective experience and the use of reason as given facts. No philosophical study is possible without this accepted point of departure. Some philosophers have tried to limit experience to the subject, deducing the subject's experience, and even deducing the structure and exigence of the subject's reasoning powers. The subject would therefore have to be absolute.

It is precisely this attempt, which is equivalent to a divinization of the self, which seems illusory and futile. We are not, in fact, self-created, nor are we the creators of the datum which the world of experience constitutes. We must make use of the world, and of our cognitive power, as something given, whose hidden potentialities and riches are gradually discovered. If we exclude identification of the conscious subject with the Absolute as something mythical—an Absolute from which the human subject has been so far separated as to have lost the memory of his own divine essence—there remains the task of seeking to learn what is implicit and previously required by this fact, this datum of experience, of which we are part and parcel, although a conscious part. It seemed evident to us that if we respect the requirement of rationality and intelligibility which is the very essence of our thinking, we would have to discern a creative Absolute as the foundation of the world, and of its development, structure, and all that it contains; an Absolute that is at least as conscious and reflective as the reflective consciousness which has appeared at the summit of the tree of life. However, experience is not merely physical, biological or even human. Within the range of experience, a new phenomenon held our attention. The fact of Israel, itself an instance of innovation, considered as a renewal of humanity, the birth of sanctity, a humanity in the image and likeness of Him who was named thrice holy by Isaias, also constitutes a creation, an achievement by which we have access to the knowledge of the hidden God, even apart from the personal manifestation of God among us: *immanu-el*.

The following passage from St. Paul's Epistle to the Romans seems especially appropriate: "Because that which is known to God is manifest in them. For God hath manifested it unto them. . . . For the invisible things of him, from the creation of the world, are clearly seen, being understood by the things that are made; his eternal power also, and divinity" (Romans 1:19–20).